Everyone should rea

DON'T GET TAKEN! . . .

Buy this book. If a penny saved is a penny earned (Ben Franklin), then *Don't Get Taken!* can save you thousands of dollars. This is not a plea to emotions, but is a call to common sense and reason. Buy it, learn it, and carry its contents with you.

Wallace I. Sampson, M.D.
Clinical Professor of Medicine, Stanford University

Not much escapes his keen eye. We have collaborated on several important projects during which I have had to depend upon his powers of observation and his inventiveness.

The victims fall for the con artists because there are not more books like this available and there are far too few Bob Steiners to fill the need.

James Randi

"The Amazing Randi"

Don't Get Taken! is a hard-hitting look at all the aspects of confidence games, old and new.

Being a law enforcement officer and having spent a great deal of time investigating and researching all types of con games, con men and women and their victims, I wholeheartedly know the importance of this quality book.

The book is great. I am adding it to my suggested reading list for students in my law enforcement seminars.

Investigator Bruce Walstad
Franklin Park (IL) Police Department
Co-author of *Sting Shift: The Street-Smart Cop's Handbook of Cons and Swindles*

Don't Get Taken! takes you through the labyrinthine world of con games and exposes the foolish but all too human ways you can be separated from your money or control over your life. Steiner's wise and trenchant book is a straight-talking, no-nonsense tough-minded approach that informs you and arms you against thievery and—with its storehouse of anecdotes—keeps you turning pages. A wonderful distillation of Steiner's decades of experience as a magician, skeptic, researcher and performer, this is a must read for anyone concerned about being taken in by the con or pure or not so pure hokum.

Michael Krasny, Ph.D.

Professor of English, San Francisco State University
Interviewer/News Commentator, ABC Radio

The facility to think critically is the most prized of all human abilities. People who con you want you to suspend your ability to think clearly. A con artist is any person who is using you without your knowledge and permission. By their nature, con artists are virtually impossible to detect. If this were not so, this book would not need to be written. If you live long enough, you will eventually be the target of a con job. Bob Steiner has written a book not as a distant observer, but as one who has spent his entire life identifying and exposing bunco and bunkum in the most unlikely of places. If the United States Congress ever passed a required reading law, this is the one book that would need to be chosen.

Terence J. Sandbek, Ph.D.

Clinical Psychologist

Bob Steiner, Past National President of The Society of American Magicians, is an expert at exposing those who use deception for committing fraud, who prey upon the unsuspecting, trusting nature of people everywhere to steal health and wealth for personal gain. *Don't Get Taken!* is a product of Steiner's love of magic and intense, passionate hatred of fraud. Much of it is drawn from actual incidents with which Bob is familiar. The book presents an excellent overview of the devious world of bunco and bunkum, which will lead you to further study and may well save you from personal grief.

Dr. David R. Goodsell, Past National President
The Society of American Magicians, Editor of *M-U-M*

Don't Get Taken! will provide a great service to law enforcement professionals and the citizens they are sworn to protect. It will save countless the embarrassment, the tragedy and the loss of their monies. It is truly a magnificent exposé on the con and bunco artist. Not to read it will be a fool's decision. Reading it will endow the reader with more street savvy and knowledge about criminal behavior characteristics than could be learned in a decade as a law enforcement officer.

The merits of this work will be the millions of dollars saved by those whose awareness of the con artists' treachery was not known prior to its reading. Cons beware! The word is now out on your sleaze and goody-two-shoes demeanor. Bravo, Mr. Steiner, you have provided the bullet to be fired at those quacks and con-artists who are out to get us all.

This book should be mandatory reading for all law enforcement personnel, as well as for every citizen who identifies with honesty and ethical behavior. It has driven a stake into the con and bunco artist's heart!

Phillip R. Derr, Sergeant
Crime Prevention Unit, San Mateo (CA) Police Department

To Ina —

With all best

wishes to a thinking

Human Being.

Bob Homer

11/2002

DON'T GET TAKEN!

Bunco and Bunkum Exposed
How to Protect Yourself

Robert A. Steiner

Wide-Awake Books
Box 659, El Cerrito
California 94530

Some names, places, and minor details have been changed, in order to protect the innocent.

First Edition, Second Printing

97 96 95 94 93 92 91 90 89   10 9 8 7 6 5 4 3 2

Library of Congress Catalog Card Number: 89-51057

ISBN 0-9623473-0-2

Manufactured in the United States of America,
a country worth saving.

To James Randi

I was fortunate to find a mentor, hero, and dear friend all in the same person.

Contents

THANK YOU!

Over the years, it has been a pleasure working with James Randi, magician, skeptic, friend, scientist, investigator, scholar, and educator.

Kent Harker, production consultant, turned my computer disks into camera-ready copy so quickly and efficiently that I feared he would finish producing this book before I finished writing it. Bart Brodsky designed the cover and the logo, and encouraged me to write the book. The cover photo was by Tom Watson.

The people who launched my public presentations deserve special recognition. Each puts forth great effort in educating the public about how to recognize and protect against bunco and bunkum.

- Professor John W. Patterson, on the university circuit.
- Wallace I. Sampson, M.D., at medical conferences and public presentations.
- Police Sergeant Phillip R. Derr, at crime prevention seminars for law enforcement and public groups.

Terence J. Sandbek, Ph.D., clinical psychologist, has been a resource of virtually unlimited understanding of why human beings do what they do.

The Committee for the Scientific Investigation of Claims of the Paranormal (CSICOP) has contributed enormously to my knowledge and action. Bay Area Skeptics has been a local support group for the study and investigation of mystical bunkum.

The Society of American Magicians has become a home for my love for magic. Joyce Zachary (National Secretary), Jim Zachary (National President 1980-1981), and David Goodsell (National President 1986-1987, and Editor of the magazine *M-U-M*) have helped cultivate my pursuit of magic. My local Assembly No. 112, of The Society of American Magicians, has produced friends, camaraderie, and a home. Jim Monsoor (Past Regional Vice President), Loren Lind (Regional Vice President), and all the others have made my association with the club a joy.

Media people have been wonderful. The excitement of being able to present controversial ideas has been stimulated by them. Especially I wish to thank Jim Eason, Michael Krasny, Dean Edell, M.D., Pete Wilson, Bob Lee, and Jim Sanders.

Mark Plummer and Dick Smith planned my undercover trip to Australia (see Chapter 3); Mark has been a sounding board on just about everything. Mensa encouraged my presentations of magic and my challenges to the mystics. Jim Letchworth took me through a (figurative) time tunnel to recreate renaissance England. Thinkest thou 'tis of little import? Thence cometh my character Merlin.

The National Council Against Health Fraud increased my awareness of bunco and bunkum in the health field. Larry Loebig and Rich Gosse have been sources of encouragement and information.

Harry Houdini was the first magician I ever heard of, and Jimmy Grippo was the first magician I ever met.

And lastly, to the first person who said to me, "Pick a card, any card": You triggered in me a lifelong passion for the entertainment art form known as *magic*. Thank you, wherever you may be.

❋ ❋ ❋ INTRODUCTION ❋ ❋ ❋

*From the mystic with the crystal ball to the psychic surgeon, from
the bogus charity operator to the phony bank examiner, from the
con artist with the fast-buck scheme to the three-card monte
operator on the corner, from coast to coast and border to border,
there are grifters (swindlers) ready to take your money. Learn how
to protect yourself.*
  Bob Steiner.

Bobby was pleased that his parents had allowed him to visit
the carnival on his own. He was 11 years old—certainly old
enough to take care of himself.

He was fascinated as he walked down the midway,
trying various games: coin-toss, knock off the bottles, bas-
ketball shooting, string game, throwing darts, hoop toss, the
wheel of fortune, and more. At none of these did he win
anything. He accepted that. He understood that he was new
at the games.

He was delighted, reveling in the joy of spending money
he had earned at his lemonade stand. He had operated that
business for two full weeks, saving every penny for the trip
to the carnival. Now he was enjoying the fruits of his labor.

Aha! Here was a game of skill right down Bobby's
alley—a puzzle. For as far back as he could remember, he
had been fascinated by puzzles—and was very good at
solving them.

The white oilcloth covering the table had a red circle
painted on it, about five inches in diameter. The operator
had five round metal disks, about three inches in diameter.
He dropped them one at a time from about three inches
above the table, seemingly casually, and completely
covered the red circle.

Bobby studied the action very carefully a couple of
times. Then he put forth his dime to give it a try. He was
sure he would go home with a handsome stuffed animal.

1

Oops! Just a tiny bit of red was showing. Another dime, another try, and another tiny bit of red showing. And again.

Bobby asked the operator to do it once more. With a warm, gentle smile, the operator obliged, assuring Bobby that one more try and he would have it. As before, the operator casually dropped the disks, completely hiding the red circle.

Bobby balked. The operator offered him three tries for a quarter. Bobby knew a bargain when he heard it, and he went for it. He was getting better. Just the tiniest bit of red was showing.

An hour passed. The operator had demonstrated several times. And Bobby handed over every penny in his possession to try this intriguing puzzle. He never covered the red spot.

Having spent his bus-fare home, he had to walk several miles. All the while on the hike home, he was thinking about how close he had come. He was frustrated that he had been unable to solve what appeared to be a fairly simple puzzle.

Decades later, a grown-up Bob would read a description of the game "spot the spot" in *The Bunco Book* (Gibson, 1946, 24-25). Only then did he learn that the carny had conned him. When it was little Bobby's turn, the operator would pull the end of the cloth just slightly. That would elongate the circle into an ellipse. Try as he might, it was then impossible for Bobby to cover the red spot.

This eleven-year-old boy had been cheated by a thieving con artist. I can almost hear his voice ringing in my ears:

> Come on, kid. You almost got it that time. You're good at this kind of thing. I can spot a winner. I knew as soon as you walked up that you would go home with a fine stuffed animal. For a quarter, I'll let you have three tries. You can do it. By the way, kid, how much money do you have left?

PART I

YOU CAN BE TAKEN

Chapter 1

"Confidence" Is the Name of the Game

The mark is not necessarily greedy, dishonest, stupid, or naive. He may just be in the right place at the wrong time.
Flim-Flam Man: How Con Games Work (Henderson 1985, 17).

You can be taken! You can be the *mark* (sucker, pigeon, victim, dupe, target, patsy, chump, rube, fall guy, gull, sap, sitting duck) of a confidence game. You can learn to trust someone who will do you wrong. He or she will appear sincere and will win your confidence. You might lose your money, your self-esteem, your health, and sometimes even your very life. These losses are the result of placing your confidence in the wrong person.

"Confidence" is the name of the game. We have all met people whom we trust and in whom we have confidence. Generally all works out well—the people are worthy of our trust and confidence.

However, some people take advantage of the normal and noble human emotion of confidence—trust in our fellow human beings. The "game" these people play is the *confidence game*. They win your confidence. Then they take your money and your self-esteem, and sometimes more.

In common jargon, *confidence game* is shortened to *con game*; the practitioners are called *con artists*. Make no mistake about it—they are criminals.

There are other people who are truly sincere, but who will still hurt you if you place your confidence in them. They are not con artists and are not criminals. They are simply misguided in their beliefs.

Let us consider astrologers, for example. (Astrology will be dealt with at length later.) For now, we wish to look at the sincerity of the practitioners. Are they sincere? Do they truly believe that the position of the earth in relation to the planets, sun, moon, and stars at the moment of your birth has influence on your personality?

Yes, many, probably most, really do believe that. But astrology has no proven scientific validity at all. It is, in a word, nonsense.

If you consult an astrologer to make life decisions, you are giving up control over your own life. You are living your life based upon mystical nonsense. That is true whether the practicing astrologer whom you consult is a fraud or a sincere true believer.

It is essential for you to understand that you can be taken in by *bunco* (fraud) and *bunkum* (nonsense).

You are vulnerable. You are not always at your peak. Even at your peak, given the proper circumstances, you can fall for a con game. Or you can follow someone who is sincere but woefully misguided.

I too am vulnerable. Given the proper set of circumstances, I can bite at a scam. I have done so.

Al Capone was certainly not a naive bumpkin. He gave $50,000 to a con artist to invest in a venture that was "guaranteed" to double the investment within two months.

Cockiness, smugness, and the arrogant self-evaluation that you are too smart to be taken will cause you to let your guard down. That, in turn, will make you more vulnerable to being the mark of some con.

I don't care how intelligent you are, how smart you are, how much you know, whom you know, how strong you are, how effectively you can fight, whether you carry a gun, how much you have read, how wealthy you are, or how much education you have had, you can be taken.

If you accept that message, you are ready to learn to recognize bunco and bunkum. That will place you in a far better position to protect yourself and those you love against these schemes. If you do not accept that message—if you think you are invulnerable—I guarantee you that you will get knocked on your pins.

Some names, places, and minor details have been changed, in order to protect the innocent. "Bob" always refers to me. Other than these cosmetic changes, the cases you will read about are true.

One final note: We will use the word *psychic* without special designation. We will not necessarily say such things as "so-called psychic" or "self-proclaimed psychic." Nor will we put the word *psychic* in quotation marks. Please understand that this is done for literary convenience. It does not mean that I believe psychics have genuine supernatural powers. That last subject will be discussed in this book.

The same positions will be taken, for the same reasons, on *psychic surgery, faith healers, blood readers,* and other such terms.

Please read on.

Chapter 2

Myths About Cons

A confidence man prospers only because of the fundamental dishonesty of his victim. . . . Thus arises the trite but nonetheless sage maxim: "You can't cheat an honest man."
   The American Confidence Man (Maurer 1974, 3-4).

FIRST, FORGET SEVERAL OLD SAWS ABOUT CHEATING AN HONEST MAN. . . . The victims of bunco, the losers, can be as pure of heart as Abraham Lincoln. . . . The con artist's victim . . . can be a lonely, aging pensioner, frightened and bewildered, senile, sometimes physically intimidated.
   A Compendium of Bunk or How to Spot a Con Artist (Carey and Sherman 1976, 3-4).

A *Myth: Con artists are gentle folk, fundamentally different from other criminals.*

   "Although [the con artist] is sometimes classed with professional thieves, he is really not a thief at all because he does no actual stealing. The trusting victim literally thrusts a fat bankroll into his hands. It is a point of pride with him that he does not have to steal" (Maurer 1976, 3).

9

In my travels I have tried, with moderate success, to learn to subdue my passions, most especially the passion of anger. I am reasonably tolerant and forgiving of ignorance. However, Professor David W. Maurer, author of *The American Confidence Man* (Maurer 1974), has tested my limits.

Maurer has done extensive research on con artists and con games. As he proudly proclaims, he went straight to the source for information: "Where, then, does one go for the answers? I have gone to the criminals themselves. And I have not been disappointed" (Maurer 1974, ix).

This learned, highly intelligent, extremely articulate professor of linguistics has studied his subject first hand. It appears that he got taken. Chapter One of his book is entitled "A Word About Confidence Men." He warmly writes about them as follows:

"The grift has a gentle touch. It takes its toll from the ripe sucker by means of the skilled hand or the sharp wit" (Maurer 1974, 3). As I read of the "gentle touch," I think of the bereaved widower who pays a psychic who pretends that she brings word from her customer's late wife, from beyond the grave.

"Of all the grifters, the confidence man is the aristocrat" (Maurer 1974, 3). I think of how "aristocratic" is the con artist who delivers a C.O.D. package to a widow, allegedly from her late husband. The con artist read the obituary column to obtain the name and address of the bereaved widow. The package contains worthless cut-up newspaper.

"Confidence men in no way resemble the popular image of the 'crook' or criminal. . . . Their depredations are very much on the genteel side" (Maurer 1974, 3). I muse about how "genteel" are the actions of the con artist who wins the confidence of a five-year-old girl walking home from school. He smiles, tells her he is her friend, and offers to buy her ice cream. She climbs into his car, and he drives away. Later he rapes her.

And lastly, Maurer explains: "I have not intended to appear as an apologist for the criminal. On the other hand, I have scrupulously refrained from passing any judgments with a moral bias" (Maurer 1974, x).

Well, the good Professor Maurer and I part paths completely. Allow me to state quite clearly: I am passing judgment. I consider con artists to be thieves, criminals, immoral, and uncivilized.

A Myth: You can't cheat an honest man.

This is heard frequently from the lips of the general public and con artists. It is not heard from informed law enforcement officers. It is flat-out false.

Professor Maurer believes the myth. See his words at the head of this chapter.

While it is true that some victims of confidence games believe they are doing something illegal, immoral, or unethical, many do not. You will read about them in the pages that follow. The senior citizen who cooperates with a phony bank examiner does so for the most noble of purposes.

A Myth: You have to be greedy in order to get taken.

This too is widely believed, and false.

Loneliness, stress, illness, grief, fear, anger, anxiety, physical pain, depression, despair, being away from home, having recently fallen in love, having recently fallen out of love, the death of a loved one, the call of civic duty, civic pride, desire to help your fellow human beings, compassion, sympathy, and many other states of mind and events can dull your judgment and make you more susceptible to a con game.

You are somewhat ripe for picking at all times. I cannot stress this too strongly.

Let us dwell just a bit more on the concept of greed. Suppose you were presented with an opportunity to make an investment, business deal, or job change that you believed would yield more money and more satisfaction to you. Upon investigation, you conclude that the deal is legal, moral, and ethical, and that no one would be hurt by it. Is there any reason why you would *on principle* turn down the deal?

Of course not. Assuming that you had done sufficient investigation and that your investigation yielded reliable results, you would be well-advised to pursue this new venture.

Then suppose that it turned out to be a con game: you lost a substantial sum of money on the venture. Many would say that you lost because you were greedy. But were you? Were you not looking out for your own legitimate self-interest? Isn't that what all of us do when we choose our investments, business deals, and jobs?

I can categorically advise you to stay away from shady deals. However, a good deal, which you have researched, and which is legitimate, is a good deal. You should, with caution and investigation, go for it.

A Myth: The practitioners of con games are properly called "con men."

I have applauded, supported, and joined with the men and women who are helping to eliminate sexist stereotypes in our language. I have appeared on feminist panels at national conventions. I believe that language can be both the cause and the result of bigotry.

Well, ladies and gentlemen, you've got to take the bad with the good.

The unconscionable acts of con artists are by no means limited to men. Many of the top and most famous con artists have been women.

A Myth: Only the stupid and the naive get taken by con artists.

A list of those who have been taken by con artists would include segments of society that would look like a "Who's Who" of Hollywood actors and actresses, government officials, otherwise astute business people, lawyers, millionaires, and of virtually every other category of human endeavor.

A Myth: If you study enough, you can absolutely protect yourself against any and all con games.

Alas, there are no guarantees. However, after reading this book, with your increased awareness, and if you apply the principles we discuss, you should be in a much better position to protect yourself and those you love against bunco and bunkum.

PART II

PSYCHICS, ASTROLOGERS, BLOOD READERS, AND OTHERS

Chapter 3

Tell 'Em What
They Want to Hear

The only thing standing between you and a million dollars is principle.
    Robert Sheaffer, to Bob Steiner, in a conversation.

You could be a millionaire. All you have to do is be a scoundrel.
    Earl Hautala, to Bob Steiner, in a conversation.

With all readings let the client interrupt and use the information he gives you to switch the reading back, saying what he desires and expects.
    Cashing in on the Psychic (Ruthchild 1978, 29- 30).

The host of the party introduced me to a staggeringly beautiful woman guest with the words, "Mary, meet Bob. Bob is a psychic."

Obviously impressed, Mary immediately requested that I tell her something about herself.

Quickly sizing up the situation, I chose my course. "You had a major fight with your boyfriend eight months ago, and you broke up with him at the time."

She replied, "I am happily married, and have been happily married for several years. My husband and I are monogamous and faithful."

Let us step back and look at that. Was that a miss on my part? Well, at first glance, it would appear to be. However, we trained psychics never give up.

"Oh, you don't wear any rings," I responded. I would not have missed rings.

Mary explained that they were at the jeweler being cleaned and polished. She quickly added, "Come to think of it, my baby was born eight months ago."

"Oh!" said I, not ready to say more, since egg was still running down my cheeks.

"Eight months ago today, as a matter of fact," she continued.

"Oh! Really!" responded I, still not quite yet ready to go forward.

"A beautiful baby boy," she intoned, as a broad smile lit up her face.

Now I was ready. "Wait a minute. I want a 99% hit. I got the exact date of birth of your baby, and I got that it was a boy."

"But," she protested, "you said that I broke up with him."

"I didn't say that," I lied, "I said that you were separated from him. They did cut the umbilical cord, didn't they?"

This woman bought the entire program. She believed. I was not surprised. I have come to expect that kind of success. The onlookers also were surprised. However, their surprise was not that she believed it. Rather, they were surprised at how "accurate" I had been.

The woman spent the next ten minutes asking everybody at the party two questions: One: Did they know the date of birth of her son? Nobody did. Two: Had they told me? Since nobody knew, no one could have told me.

She spent some of the remainder of the party telling everybody of remarkable psychic Bob Steiner who had told her the exact date of birth of her baby, and that it was a son.

If I had been a practicing psychic, if I had been inclined to follow up on my reading, at that point I virtually owned this woman. She asked me for an appointment for a private psychic reading. If I had chosen to pursue it, she would have paid me handsomely for psychic readings and advice.

Spoilsport that I am, I later explained to her how I had tricked her. It took some patience and perseverance on my part to convince her. She really wanted to believe and did believe that I was psychic. She truly believed that I had told her what in fact she had told me.

I hear partial stories like the above all the time. People tell me the wondrous, accurate information given by a psychic, and demand that I explain how it could have been done.

Sometimes I cannot answer. If a woman came to me and told me that a psychic at a party had told her the exact date of birth of her son, and that she had never met the psychic, and that no one else at the party knew the date of birth of her son, I would not have a ready explanation. I was not there, so I did not hear the manipulations of the reader.

My reputation for being able to convince people that I am psychic had spread quite far. In 1984, I accepted the offer of an all-expense-paid trip to Australia, where I posed as astonishing psychic Steve Terbot. I appeared on prime-time television and radio, was written up in newspapers and magazines, and had people running after me in the streets, asking for autographs and information about their lives, future, love affairs, jobs, health, travel, and more.

At the Ringwood Cultural Centre (in Ringwood, Victoria, Australia), having done some psychic demonstrations, I was taking questions from the audience. A woman asked me to do more readings on audience members.

I inquired, "How many of you would like private readings, understanding that I will charge for them?" More than one hundred hands were raised. If I had been inclined to take them up on it, I could have earned thousands of dollars in the matter of a few days. Then they would have come back, and would have encouraged their friends and relatives to see amazing psychic Steve Terbot.

However, I have never done readings for pay by the persons on whom I did the readings. Furthermore, I have never done readings where I did not later explain that it was a fake, a hoax. Yes, I have been hired by universities to give presentations in which I pose as a psychic. I convince most of the audience that I am psychic, and then reveal the hoax.

Back to Ringwood Cultural Centre.

I looked directly at the woman who had made the inquiry and confidently asserted, "You want me to do a reading on you."

Shocked, she replied, "Yes!"

"You are thinking about your brother or sister."

She inquired, "Which one? I have several brothers and sisters."

I replied, "The one you have not heard from in three months."

Visibly shaken with my perceptive, detailed knowledge, she came back with, "Which one, my brother or my sister?"

I boldly stated, "Your brother."

The woman weakened with emotion. Her voice softened and quivered as she inquired, "Yes. Is he all right?"

I quickly assured her, "Yes. He is fine. He will call you next week."

"Oh, thank you," she said, as she took her seat.

Later, a skeptic in the audience attacked me by saying, "Everything this bloke did a skilled magician could do."

The woman immediately stood up in my defense and firmly assured everyone, "No! No magician could have told me what he told me about my brother."

Since all of the advance promotion for this event was about "Steve Terbot, Psychic," the audience consisted primarily of believers. With the exception of the handful who were in on the hoax, I estimate that about 95% were believers and 5% were skeptics. Of the skeptics, I estimate that the vast majority believed that either this woman was a plant or that I had done advance research. None of the believers and evidently few of the skeptics understood the workings of a *cold reading.*

In fact, it was all a cold reading. In a cold reading, the mystic—that can be a psychic, astrologer, phrenologist, palmist, numerologist, or any of numerous other mystical practitioners of nonsense—starts cold, with no information. The reader begins with generalities which are applicable to large segments of the population. He or she pays careful attention to reactions: words, body language, skin color, breathing patterns, dilation or contraction of the pupils of the eye, and more. The subject of the reading will usually convey important information to the reader: sometimes in words, and sometimes in bodily reactions to the reading.

From observation, the reader will feed back to the subject what the latter wants to hear. That is the overwhelming guiding principle of the mystics: Tell 'em what they want to hear. That will keep them coming back for more.

Let us look more closely at my cold reading of the woman in the Cultural Centre.

When she inquired about whether I would do more readings, it was obvious that she wanted me to do a reading on her.

When I said that she was thinking about her brother or sister, that is one of the broad generalities on which cold readings are based. If she had neither brother nor sister, perhaps (only perhaps) I would have had to escape to another approach, such as: "All your life you have thought about how it would be to have a brother or a sister." That is certainly a safe statement to make to an only child.

Her reply was that she had several brothers and sisters. Look at all the information she gave me.

From several brothers and sisters, it was enormously likely that there was one whom she had not heard from in several months. Saying "three months" made it appear that I had precise knowledge. It was unlikely that she would remember the exact amount of time since she had heard from her sibling. Subjects try very hard to make the mystic be correct. They will search and scan their memories to make my broad generalities fit what they know to be the facts in their lives.

In her next question, she said "brother" first, so I went with brother. Among several siblings, had I said "sister," she probably would have searched through her sisters to find one she had not heard from in a while. However, "brother" came first from her, so I went with that.

And finally, when she expressed concern about the brother she had not heard from in months, what did she want to hear? Obviously she wanted to hear precisely what I told her, "He is fine. He will call you next week."

At the conclusion of the readings and performance, I refused to schedule any private readings. I told them all to be sure to watch The Bert Newton Show next Thursday. *Tonight With Bert Newton* (Channel 9 Network) was the prime time television show on which I had appeared three times. On the first two, I had convinced literally millions of people that I was psychic.

At the time of the presentation at the Cultural Centre, the third appearance on the Bert Newton Show was upcoming. We were scheduled to present, and did present, a full exposé and explanation of the entire hoax we had played upon the very nice people in Australia. Mark Plummer (then National President of Australian Skeptics, now Executive Director of The Committee for the Scientific Investigation of Claims of the Paranormal) and Dick Smith (patron of Australian Skeptics) had each seen me perform in the United States. They conceived the idea of flying me to Australia to deliver a message.

The message, in which the fine, courageous folks at *Tonight With Bert Newton* participated, was to warn the people of Australia to beware of people claiming to be psychic. I had done what many others had done in the past, with only two differences: 1) I told them that I was a fake, and 2) I did not take one penny from anyone who believed that I was a psychic.

Listen to me, and I will tell you about you. Pretend that I am an astrologer, a psychic, a tarot reader, a palm reader, or any other such person. You came to me for advice. Listen.

I see that you are very frank and forthright in dealing with people. Sometimes that backfires on you. You kick yourself, and tell yourself that you were too open, and that you should have kept your mouth shut. However, on balance, that is a very good and honorable trait. Don't try to change it. But be aware that it will sometimes backfire.

You have a great deal of unused capacity. You find yourself bogged down with details. That prevents you from accomplishing some useful goals. You are pretty good at scheduling your time. However, sometimes you look back at the past hour or two and find that you have merely shuffled papers or were daydreaming.

You have had some minor sexual difficulties. It was nothing serious. You have been able to overcome it, although there were some minor adjustments necessary in your overall thinking. Right now, except for a minor trivial nagging on one aspect, you feel substantially secure in your sexual outlook.

I see that you are advancing toward a goal or some goals you had set for yourself a while back. Oh yes, I see some setbacks. It has been two or three steps forward, and one step back. Keep your eye on the ball, and you will find success and happiness.

Now, honestly, how did I do? If you had come to me for information, would you have been satisfied? Be aware, had you come to me as a believer seeking guidance in your life, you would have been feeding back information long before I reached the end of the reading, much as the woman did as she directed me to her brother.

On two television shows, competing against psychics, I have won. Each time there were two full-time, "professional," practicing psychics. Each of us gave demonstrations of psychic readings. The audience was told that there were three psychics. Both times I was ranked to be best.

For a television investigative report (Edell 1989), members of a studio audience were invited to have private readings by a psychic. Each of twelve volunteers got a private reading by me, posing as a psychic. Twelve out of twelve answered a questionnaire indicating belief in mind reading, and all twelve clearly stated their belief that I have psychic powers. That was a 100% success rate.

The mystics claim to do their readings by using psychic powers or specialized knowledge. I do my readings by using study, planning, and trickery. The subjects have consistently expressed the belief that I am psychic or have specialized knowledge. Why on earth should I believe that the mystics have any special powers or knowledge? And why should you?

Chapter 4

Are Psychics Real?

Most of the time even a pseudo mind reading trick will convince the believer that you are real. . . . Believers look for something paranormal in which to believe. They will grasp even the most blatant phonies for proof that there is something more. These people are growing in number. They are waiting for you. They want to believe you.
    Cashing in on the Psychic (Ruthchild 1978, 24).

And so hundreds of people who waited upon my spirits for advice in marital, legal, medical, and other problems of their lives built their existence here and the hope of a future one hereafter on a mere magician's bag of tricks!
    The Psychic Mafia (Keene 1976, 91).

"**P**arapsychology is the study of psychic or *psi* phenomena (pronounced 'sigh')" (Auerbach 1986, 15). "We have no central theory of psi functioning. There, I've said it, plain and simple" (Auerbach 1986, 97).

Loyd Auerbach, parapsychological consultant, is the author of *ESP, Hauntings and Poltergeists: A Parapsy-*

chologist's Handbook (Auerbach 1986). He is personally known to me: He is intelligent, articulate, sincere, and, in my opinion, substantially on the wrong track in his views. To the obvious dismay of people on both sides of the aisle, Loyd and I are good friends.

He explains his field of study as follows:

> Parapsychology is a field of science (a beginning field some have labeled a "protoscience") with no coherent viewpoint to tie all the phenomena together and to explain the way we think it all works. . . . We have no workable mechanism to place psychic functioning in the universe the way science sees it running. Not yet (Auerbach 1986, 97-98).

Any dictionary will tell you that "psychic" refers to extrasensory or supernatural phenomena. Further, it will explain that it is outside the realm of the normal or what can be explained by science.

Uri Geller, stellar performer of the psychic world, has been exposed as using trickery quite explicitly and thoroughly in several works. For the definitive word on Geller, I heartily recommend for your reading enjoyment *The Truth About Uri Geller*, by James Randi (Randi [1975] 1982).

Several friends and I attended a performance by Geller in San Francisco a few years ago. Not only could I duplicate every single feat that he performed, but I had done every single one of them in my past shows. There was, however, one significant difference: I did not claim that they were done by supernatural, mystical, or psychic powers.

Outside the theater, after the show, several activists in Bay Area Skeptics were passing out literature. One woman was quite upset by our activities. She challenged me by saying that Geller had done things that normal human beings could not do. I inquired what those things were. She replied, "Bending a key."

I requested that she give me her keys. As soon as she had done so, I immediately placed them back in her hand, with the instruction that she close her hand. I told her male friend to rub her hand, and instructed both of them to think "BEND!"

I inquired whether she could feel a key bending. She replied, "No."

I said, "Well, I guess it did not work."

Triumphant and indignant, she proclaimed loudly, "See that! If what you claim were true, you would have been able to bend a key. But you could not!"

When she opened her hand, she observed that one of her keys was bent at a 45 degree angle. She let out a shriek that could be heard a block away. However, she quickly recovered her composure and rose to defend Geller, "But you did it by a trick."

"Of course I did it by a trick," I replied.

Quickly she responded with, "But Geller does it psychically."

I inquired whether she had seen me bend the key. She admitted that she had not. I inquired whether she had seen Geller bend the key. She admitted that she had not.

I then summed it all up, "Oh, I see. Your personal observation was identical in both cases: you did not see me bend the key and you did not see Geller bend the key. But you know that I did it by trickery because I told you I did it by trickery, and you know that Geller did it by using psychic powers because he told you he uses psychic powers."

"That's right!" she replied confidently.

"You lose!" said her escort, quite correctly, as he pointed at me.

M. Lamar Keene, author of *The Psychic Mafia* (Keene 1976), had been one of the most successful practitioners of the psychic con game in the world. Finally, he could take it no longer. He summoned up a considerable amount of courage and blew the whistle: he told all. He pulled no punches in his exposé. We read such revelations as:

> In my days as a medium I had sat in on meetings at which were discussed various means of expediting the demise of certain elderly folk who were sure to leave a lot of money to the spiritualist cause. One woman medium claimed to be an expert in poisons that were virtually untraceable (Keene 1976, 153).

Miriam Ruthchild, in her book *Cashing in on the Psychic*, offers the following advice to students wishing to cash in on the psychic:

> Whether you believe in E.S.P. [extrasensory perception] and psychic powers or not, you must constantly act like you do in public. This is not like any other entertainment skill. You must constantly impress people with your belief. It is a cloak that you don and can never take off while you are in the public. . . . You never know who is around when you are in public. You can always be overheard. You are on stage at all times. Never let your mask slip (Ruthchild 1978, 19).
>
> Even if you consider it a con or game, it must never appear that way to the public. . . . Never admit disbelief, even to your closest friend. It works. That is your every thought. Your credibility depends upon it (Ruthchild 1978, 23).

Sincere, careful researchers in the field of parapsychology cause no problem. Sloppy researchers, dishonest researchers (some have been caught faking data), con artists (as M. Lamar Keene was in his practitioner days), and gullible and/or careless media reporters team up to give psychics an air of respectability which is not deserved.

Of course, true believers are the mainstay of this type of bunkum: people who believe based upon an unshakable faith. They are the people who support the mystics.

The term "true believer" was analyzed and brought to public attention by Eric Hoffer in 1951, in his masterful work *The True Believer* (Hoffer 1951). For an understanding of what drives people and movements into the frenzy we observe about us, I recommend Hoffer's book.

For further reading that details the careless, outright sloppy research that has been conducted in the field of parapsychology, I recommend the items in the Bibliography referenced as: Randi [1980] 1982, Marks and Kammann 1980, Hansel 1980, Kurtz 1985, Gardner 1981, Abell and Singer 1981, Christopher 1970, Christopher 1975, and CSICOP. *The Skeptical Inquirer* is an excellent quarterly journal published by The Committee for the Scientific Investigation of Claims of the Paranormal (CSICOP). It covers the spectrum of mystical and paranormal claims. Try it.

Many people are quite sensitive and perceptive. I use the words *sensitive* and *perceptive* in the normal sense. For example, a woman might have met you a year ago on the beach. Last night, when you met again at a party, she recognized you, called you by name, reminded you where you met, and described the color and style swimsuit you were wearing.

This ability to pick up subtle clues surprises most people, including the person who picks them up. The astonishment of others will frequently lead to comments of "You must be psychic!" Hearing that enough, the person begins to believe that he or she is indeed psychic.

Some, and I venture to say most, of the people who claim that they have psychic ability are sincere, but are in error. A minority are dedicated, conscious frauds.

Psychic powers are often made to appear to work on performing stages and in private and public readings of people. Allow me to leave you with knowledge of the three places where claimed psychic ability does not work: in the scientific laboratory where there are proper scientific controls, in gambling (at the racetrack, gaming tables, and the lottery), and in the stock market.

Regardless of the grandiose claims you may have read, seen, or heard from the media or psychic performers, the existence of psychic phenomena has not been validated by properly controlled scientific testing. Belief in psychic phenomena is, as of this writing, based exclusively upon faith, misperception, misinterpretation, and/or outright deception (including self-deception).

I have no quarrel with those who wish to pursue the hypothesis of its existence through careful scientific inquiry. However, to accept as a conclusion that it exists, to base your life decisions upon the claims of its practitioners, is wasteful, foolhardy, and dangerous.

Don't get taken!

Chapter 5

Do Psychics Help The Police?

I get a man, black. I hear screaming, screaming. I'm running up stairs and down. My head . . . someone bounces my head on the wall or floor. I see trees—a park? In the city, but green. Did this person live there? What does the number "2" mean? I get a bad, bloody taste in my mouth. The names "John" or "Joseph" or something like that. I am running on the street like a crazy. I can't hold the envelope in my hand.

   "An Evaluation of the Use of Psychics in the Investigation of
   Major Crimes" (Reiser et al. 1979, 19).

We have all heard reports claiming that psychics help the police in solving crimes. "Attempts to verify these reports with the police agencies mentioned have been unsuccessful to date" (Reiser et al. 1979, 18).

Psychologists with the Los Angeles Police Department teamed up with an associate professor of psychology at Los

31

Angeles City College to conduct a scientific test of the usefulness of information provided by psychics. The results were written up in the *Journal of Police Science and Administration* (Reiser et al. 1979).

Twelve psychics were set to work to provide information useful to the solving of four crimes. That is a total of 48 attempts.

The response above "provided by one participant illustrates the type of information which the researchers had to evaluate against known facts. . . . This response, though briefer than some, is representative in content to numerous responses of other psychics" (Reiser et al. 1979, 19).

That is typical of what psychics do in most of their endeavors. They speak in broad generalities, subject to far-flung interpretations. Then, after the correct information becomes known, they, together (alas) with the media, reinterpret what they said and what they meant in order to make the psychic impressions fit the later-discovered facts.

For example, if the criminal had been named James, and if he had lived at 682 Main Street in a second-floor walk-up, I guarantee you that the psychic quoted above would have claimed a direct hit on three counts: the name, the address, and the stairs.

How did these psychics do in this scientific test?

> Overall, little, if any, information was elicited from the twelve participants that would provide material helpful in the investigation of the major crimes in question. There was a low rate of inter-psychic congruence and accuracy among the responses elicited in this research. We are forced to conclude, based on our results, that the usefulness of psychics as an aid in criminal investigation has not been validated (Reiser et al. 1979, 23-24).

Yet the clamoring of the public demanding that police follow the inane claims and useless information of psychics continues unabated.

Some time ago, I was the guest on a radio talk show in Iowa. I neither lived nor worked in Iowa. The very first exposure to the information provided was given to me while I was being interviewed on the air. I had no time for research or investigation. Throughout all of Iowa, people were virtually worshiping a psychic who had "found the body" of a murder victim. The host of the show asked me to explain how the psychic was able to find the body.

Armed with no knowledge of the case, and having no time to prepare, I conducted a live investigation on the air. The conversation went approximately as follows:

RS (me): You say the psychic found the body?

Host: Yes.

RS: I see. The psychic went to the police station and requested that they drive her to where the body was. As they drove, she told them what streets to take and where to turn. Is that the way it happened?

Host: Well, not exactly. She was not actually there when the body was found.

RS: Oh. Then she simply gave the exact address and location of the body, and the police went there at her instruction. Is that what happened?

Host: Well, no, it was not quite like that. And the police were not the ones who found the body.

RS: Please tell me what she said and what happened.

Host: She said the body would be found near running water. Two weeks later, two hunters found the body at the edge of a river.

RS: Aha! Now I understand. She pinpointed where the body would be found. Even though the exact location was not given, it was precise enough that she could justifiably claim a direct hit.

The host got excited at that, finally believing that I understood and accepted the "miraculous abilities" of the psychic. He exclaimed, "Yes, now you've got it!"

RS: So all she said was that the body would be found near running water. Her description of the location was no more precise than that.

Host: Yes, but the body was found near the edge of the river. How do you explain that?

RS: Suppose, instead of at the edge of the river, the body had been found in the man's own home, under the cellar steps, right near the water pipes. Would that have qualified as being "near running water"?

Host (reluctantly): Well, yes, I suppose so.

RS: If the body had been found in a sewer, would that have qualified as being near running water?

Host (more reluctantly): Well, yes.

RS: How about in the baseball park, near the water fountain?

Host (with a tone of begging for mercy): Yes. Give me a break.

RS: Where in Iowa do people live that is not near running water?

The psychic had made the broad, sweeping generalization about where the body would be found: near running water. She did not name the water, the location, or even that it would be near a river. Then, when the body was found near the river, she *and the media* jumped all over it and gave her a direct hit.

Whether she was a con artist or a naive true believer, her actions following the discovery of the body are understandable. However, for the media to jump all over such a case is unforgivable. In their heart of hearts, they know better, and they owe fairer, more accurate reporting to the general public. The public relies upon the media to be professional in their investigations and reporting.

Some years ago, in Atlanta, Georgia, many children were murdered. The hunt for the killer went on unsuccessfully for years. Several world-renowned psychics flocked to Atlanta, amidst great fanfare, to solve the crimes and to help the police. None of them gave the slightest bit of help in solving the crimes.

Yielding to the pleas of the public to leave no stone unturned, the police were forced to follow the many and contradictory babbling "clues" of a gaggle of psychics. The time, money, and wasted professional time and energy lost through this useless, nonsensical demand by the public is incalculable.

Psychics claim that they help the police, the media reports that the psychics help the police, and the public is taken in. Your tax dollars and your safety from harm are both sacrificed in this useless pursuit.

Your local police deserve your support. They protect you from harm in so many ways. They put their lives on the line to do their job.

Help them to do their job unfettered by the pursuit of the unproven and the irrational. If it becomes an issue in your town, speak out against shackling our local law enforcement officers in the chains of bunkum.

Chapter 6

Astrology Is Bigotry

Bigotry, n. Prejudgment of a person based upon an accident of birth over which the person has no control, and which has no scientific validity.

Bob Steiner.

The above seems to be a reasonable working definition of *bigotry* as it regards the prejudgment of human beings by human beings.

When one person evaluates another for a job, jury selection, criminal guilt, membership in an association, or any of several other areas of life based upon the color of the person's skin, the person's religion, or the color of the person's eyes, there is a storm of protest. "Bigotry! Racism!" are the cries.

And yet, when one human evaluates the worth of another based upon an accident of birth—the date of birth, it is accepted. It is called *astrology*.

Friends, astrology is bigotry. That is a clear, demonstrable fact.

At issue in our discussion of astrology is not whether astrology is bigotry. Astrology *is* bigotry. Rather, we are addressing whether you wish to defend bigotry, whether you wish to base your life on bigotry.

Practitioners, some of whom are frauds and most of whom are sincere, cast horoscopes—fancy charts devoid of useful meaning. They profess to interpret the horoscopes, in order to gather and dispense great wisdom.

In repeated scientific tests to attempt to validate its efficacy, the bunkum called astrology has failed miserably.

Is astrology a science? No. It is, at the most fundamental level, based upon magical thinking. An example of magical thinking is the principle of correspondences. The planet Mars is red; blood is red. Therefore, so the nonsense of magical thinking would go, someone born with Mars in the horoscope is impulsive, hot-tempered, and prone to fighting.

Is there a force that causes the planets to have an influence on people? No. None has been demonstrated or measured, or even defined.

Could the force be gravity? No. The gravitational force of the hospital building acting upon the newborn infant is greater than the gravitational force of all the planets and stars together, save only the sun and moon.

Many, in ignorance, point to experiments by Michel Gauquelin as "proof" of astrology. Before you even consider accepting that argument, consider the words of Dr. Gauquelin himself, in his book *Dreams and Illusions of Astrology*:

> The horoscope is a product that is bought and sold, and that leads people to dreams. But the dreams of the clientele are answered by the deceptions of the charlatan, as well as by the illusions of the researcher who is sincere but not very lucid.
>
> This psychological reality is based on a firmly rooted scientific error. As interesting as it may be, the origin of astrology was developed on mythological bases that are not at all compatible with modern scientific objectivity. And especially, serious scientific examination is never favorable to this ancient doctrine. . . . The horoscope is certainly a commercial reality, but it is a scientific illusion, or rather just an illusion (Gauquelin 1979, 157).

Please note that Dr. Gauquelin recognizes the contribution of both bunco and bunkum to the perpetuation of this nonsense. To continue:

> Today, the roller of charlatanism, disguised in the tinselled finery of modern technology, represents a psychological and social danger. And since the most painstaking studies have shown the inanity of horoscopes, there should be a strong rising up against this exploitation of public credulity. Unfaithful even to the cosmic dreams of antiquity and dangerous to the honest researcher, this exploitation dishonors those who practice it. This is why commercial astrology and its charlatans must be struggled against.
>
> The sorcerer gave way to the doctor, even in the mind of the general public; at the dawn of the age of interplanetary travel, it is time that the fortune teller leave the stage in his turn, and be replaced by a new man of science (Gauquelin 1979, 158).

Amen.

Chapter 7

Hitler Was an Aries

[Those born under the sign of Aries] can't lie worth a tinker.
Linda Goodman's Sun Signs (Goodman 1968, 5).

The great masses of the people . . . will more easily fall victims to a
big lie than to a small one.
Adolf Hitler (Hitler 1933, vol. I, ch. 10).

Before dismissing astrology out of hand, most assuredly we should acquaint ourselves with the characteristics that are attributed to us. We should also see with whom we share our birth signs.

Linda Goodman's Sun Signs (Goodman 1968) has sold millions of copies. From that we surmise that she is an authority on astrology. In her book, for each sign, she has a section on "How to Recognize [that sign]." We will take a quote from here and a snippet from there, in order that you may learn about either 1) yourself and your characteristics, or (*not* and) 2) the inconsistency and contradictions of this

41

ancient wisdom called astrology. Please understand that
what we point out in Goodman's book is not unique. Rather,
it is representative of what you will find in most books
touting astrology, as well as in most books selling other
mystical bunkum.

All quotations in the remainder of this chapter are from
Linda Goodman's Sun Signs (Goodman 1968); citations are
page numbers.

ARIES the Ram, March 21st through April 20th.

- The ram is conscious only of himself (4).

- His needs come first (4).

- Aires is concerned with the world only as it
  relates to himself (5).

- You can look for a liberal attitude, lavish
  generosity with both time and material things
  (6).

- There's little that's graceful about the ram (6).

- The ram can also be the epitome of social grace
  (10).

Are you getting the idea that if you read enough you
will run across virtually all facets of all behavior patterns?
Bingo! The above contradictions are separated in Goodman's text, so that you will not stumble upon them without
some effort. That is what attracts people to astrology in the
first place: the idea that they can get simple and immediate
answers to life's complex problems without effort.

You will be pleased to know that you share your birth
sign with Adolf Hitler.

TAURUS the Bull, April 21st through May 21st.

- The most fertile places to look for him would be
  a farm, a bank, or a real estate office (46).

- You'll also find him grazing in other pastures.
  There are Taurean engineers, movie stars,
  clerks, gardeners, kings and queens, chimney
  sweeps, butchers, bakers and candlestick makers
  (46).

Well that sure narrows down the field for you.

- Like Gibraltar, he is solid and steady and
  nothing disturbs his tranquility (46).
- When the bull gets mad, he can destroy
  everything in his path. . . . Destroy is not the
  right word. Demolish is better. It may be some
  time before the dust settles and peace reigns
  again (47).

Now that you know exactly where to find a Taurus and
have a precise understanding about said person's temperament regarding anger, let us give you a detailed, specific
description of what he or she looks like. Ready?

- It's true that they frequently have large,
  generous bodies, ranging from muscular to
  plump to fat (48).

Got it? But wait! There is more.

- But if you get that image too set in your mind,
  you won't recognize the skinny ones, and it's
  important to learn to spot them, too (48).

Now let me see if I can make your day: You share your
birth sign with Jim Jones, of Peoples Temple, Jonestown,
Guyana fame.

Rather than burden you with additional pages covering
the remaining ten signs, allow me simply to assure you that
the same inane drivel continues throughout all of them. One
final example should lock in that idea.

- Scorpio [who shares the birth sign with Paul Joseph Goebbels and Charles Manson] likes to travel incognito. Thanks to his well-controlled nature, he usually succeeds (278).

- There's a crackling, electric vitality about the very presence of a Scorpio that gives him away (279).

Chapter 8

The Blood Readers

A revolutionary breakthrough in personality analysis!

"The latest craze. . . . What's in our veins reveals much more about our character than what's in our stars." —People.
     You Are Your Blood Type (Nomi and Besher [1983] 1988, cover).

There seems to be no end to the proliferation of nonsense. Published in Japan in 1983, translated into English and published in the United States of America in 1988, *You Are Your Blood Type* (Nomi and Besher [1983] 1988) splashed on the scene with yet another "revolutionary breakthrough" in the selling of balderdash to an eager and gullible public.

All quotations in this chapter are from *You Are Your Blood Type*; citations are page numbers.

Co-author Alexander Besher wastes no time getting our attention. By the second paragraph of the Preface, he has already described "this brilliant and lovely Japanese

experimental movie director" (11) Kimiko. He did not
waste a whole lot of time getting to the important things
with her, either. By the end of that second paragraph in the
Preface, we are informed that he landed on her on their first
date. And then, guess what? You've got it—they discussed
their blood types.

The exciting second paragraph of the Preface concludes
with:

> Afterwards [after you-know-what], while sipping iced
> Russian vodka on my deck overlooking the expanse of
> lights that Los Angeles becomes at night, Kimiko told
> me that she wanted to share a personal secret. "It's the
> first time I have been with an AB," she said. "But I
> knew it would make both of us very happy" (11).

Claiming not to know his own blood type, Besher tells
us that he later learned that Kimiko was correct—he does
indeed have type AB blood.

If you search the book seeking citations of studies
proving their hypothesis, you will come up empty. We find
only such things as:

- The walls in Toshitaka Nomi's office are
  plastered with graphs and charts showing the
  state of various studies being conducted at any
  given time (12-13).

- If the Japanese are taking blood-type analysis
  seriously, it is probably worthy of contemplation
  (21).

- They laughed at Newton! (21).

So much for the scientific evidence and documentation.
Now they get to the practical uses of this hokum. For
example, you might use it as a pick-up line. Thinkest thou
that I jest? Nay. Nay. Forsooth, 'twas in this wondrous book,
to wit:

> Just imagine walking up to an attractive stranger and
> starting up a conversation. "Excuse me," you begin,

secure in your knowledge that you are applying one of the most innovative opening lines in modern times. "I was wondering what your blood type is. I thought you might be an A by the way you looked at the details in that Fra Angelico, but I'm not sure" (21).

In a manner similar to the astrologers, the blood readers tell you the important people with whom your share your blood type. For example, President Dwight David Eisenhower, President Ronald Reagan, Nobel Prize-winning physicist Murray Gell-Mann, and Lynn Redgrave all have blood type O.

Get ready for an important piece of news: "Most of the big Mafiosi [members of the Mafia] are members of the O blood group" (45).

We have come to an extremely important lesson in learning to recognize bunkum. Frequently it does not take any specific scientific knowledge on your part, nor does it necessarily require familiarity with the subject. Rather, if you simply apply some common sense to the claims, the tomfoolery will jump out at you.

Suppose you wanted to learn the blood types of "most of the big Mafiosi." Where would you begin? Would you go to your local library and ask to see *The Directory of Big Mafiosi*? Do you think such a directory exists? Do you think such a list exists anywhere?

Let us assume that somehow you were able to obtain a list of "the big Mafiosi." What is your next step? Ah yes, the survey:

Dear Mr. _____:

In conducting a survey of the Big Mafiosi, it has come to our attention that you are a Big Mafioso. We would appreciate your cooperation in answering just three simple questions. The first two questions are for the purpose of verifying that you are properly in our survey. The third question is the subject of the survey. Please put an "X" next to the correct answers:

1. I hereby admit in writing that I am a member of the Mafia: Yes____ No____.

2. Furthermore, I am considered to be a Big Mafioso:
                                        Yes____ No____.

3. My blood type is: O____ A____ B____ AB____.

If you do not know your blood type, we respectfully request that you see your physician, in order to learn it. While we know that your time is valuable, and while we hate to inconvenience you, we consider this survey to be quite important.

Thank you very much for your cooperation.

The assertion made by the authors about the blood types of the "big Mafiosi" is *nonfalsifiable*. That is, there is no way that you could obtain the information to show that their assertion is incorrect. There is no way you could falsify it.

If it is not falsifiable, then it is not a scientific claim. We will discuss falsifiability in more detail later.

Additionally, we did not have to dig far to learn that their statement might be reasonably correct. In their own book they state that "more people are Os than any other type" (39).

Now let us look at the claimed personality of blood type O people. As with my analysis of the traits of the astrological signs, the contradictory characteristics are all there. You will find whatever applies to you:

• Clear-sighted

• Can lose perspective

• Realistic

• Escapes from reality when troubled

- Can treat superiors well
- Can't follow too well

- Positive, idealistic
- Tramples the less fortunate (49).

I was all ready to put away *You Are Your Blood Type* and move on when some goodies in the chapter "The Type AB Personality" caught my eye. They are too much fun to pass up:

> Is it any surprise then that the most illustrious AB in history was Jesus Christ? Christ was identified as an AB type through chemical analysis of blood stains on the famous Shroud of Turin. . . . Amazingly, the shroud has withstood the most stringent scientific scrutiny. Some experts examining it have concluded that it may well be the shroud that was used to wrap the body of Jesus Christ following his execution on the cross (75).

Read the words carefully: "*Some* experts examining it have concluded that it *may well be.* . . ."

It may interest you to know that *at no time* did any significant portion of the scientific community accept the Shroud of Turin as being the shroud of Jesus Christ. As of now, it has been totally discredited. It was an elaborate hoax. It was not the shroud of Jesus Christ.

One more:

> Unfortunately, the blood types of other great religious leaders remain unknown. But the odds are that the founders of the world's greatest religions like the Gautama Buddha, Mohammed, and mystics from St. Francis to Mahatma Gandhi were likely AB types (75).

Do you wonder how they computed those odds? Well, I did, so I did a little arithmetic.

When they say "mystics from St. Francis to Mahatma Gandhi," we may presume that perhaps they meant to include several in between. However, in order to bend over backwards to be fair to these authors, let us assume that section includes only St. Francis and Mahatma Gandhi. With that assumption, they named four persons of unknown blood type who "were likely AB types."

According to their book, "The rarest of the four blood types, AB people make up only four percent of the American population" (74). While the proportion of blood types might vary from country to country, for want of a better figure, let us go with their four percent figure.

The probability of those four specific persons of unknown blood type all being type AB is four percent to the fourth power. That means that when they say that "the odds are" and that those folks all "were likely AB types," they are referring to a probability of less than three in one million (less than 3 in 1,000,000).

Think about that. With their careless and completely unfounded and unsupported assertion, stating as an odds-on favorite and likely an event which has a probability of less than three in one million, how reliable do you consider their other completely unsupported assertions?

Chapter 9

And Others

You're too stubborn, too arrogant, and too pigheaded to admit that the Ouija board worked through you!
    Said to me at a party.

The scene was a party at the home of friends of friends. I was an out-of-town guest. They were very gracious people. They believed in the Ouija board. We were seated around the kitchen table. As they were working this mystical, nonsensical board, I proceeded to call out instructions. "Your knees are supposed to be touching." The two operators at the board adjusted their positions so that their knees touched. "Sit up taller." Obediently following directions, they stiffened their postures, raising themselves a few inches. "Hold your hands a little more lightly on the planchette."

I was immediately recognized and accepted as an expert. Most people call that thing "the pointer," "the hand" (it is shaped like a hand, frequently with a picture of a hand

51

on it), or simply "that thing." My knowledge that it is properly called a "planchette" marked me as an authority. They requested that I sit at the Ouija board. After allowing them to plead a bit, I accepted the request.

"Is there a presence that wants to make itself known?" Such was the incantation uttered by me, as my hands and the hands of another rested lightly on the planchette. The planchette glided gracefully across the Ouija board, pausing to point at various letters, carefully spelling the name "Jonathan." The hostess let out a shriek, "That's my nephew! Ask the Ouija board if it means my nephew."

Again I appealed to the Ouija board for information: "Is there another presence that wants to make itself known?" The board happily responded by spelling "Sheryl." The hostess exclaimed, "That's my niece!"

Our gracious hostess knew as an absolute certainty that neither I nor anyone else there knew the names of her nephew Jonathan and niece Sheryl. We sat in the kitchen for twenty minutes discussing how it was possible for the Ouija board to come up with such precise, accurate information.

I told them it was a trick. They assured me that it could not possibly have been a trick. Since I was from out of town, they were certain that I could not possibly have obtained the information. As the discussion got a bit heated, someone blurted out in my direction, "You're too stubborn, too arrogant, and too pigheaded to admit that the Ouija board worked through you!"

After twenty minutes of discussion and searching, I decided that it was time to relieve them of their pain. I referred them to two 8-1/2 x 11" pictures on the kitchen wall about five feet away from where we were seated. They were obviously drawn by little children. Printed neatly under one picture, in inch-high letters, was the name Jonathan; under the other was neatly printed the name Sheryl.

Doing readings on people is a form of breaking and entering. Unlike the burglar who breaks and enters your home, store, factory, or office, the mystical reader seemingly breaks and enters into your thoughts.

Tarot cards are the forerunner of the playing cards which we now use in games such as poker, bridge, and the like. To "read fortunes," the tarot cards are shuffled, laid out, and interpreted by the reader. An instruction book gives you the following guidelines:

> It should be remembered that the cards must be interpreted relatively to the subject, which means that all official and conventional meanings of the cards may and should be adapted to harmonize with the conditions of this particular case in question—the position, time of life and sex of the . . . person for whom the consultation is made.
>
> *The Pictorial Key to the Tarot* (Waite 1971, 287, 294, 309).

As you can readily see, the tarot cards are just the mystical trappings, the window dressing for the reading. The reading itself is adapted to the subject paying for the reading. In this respect, reading of tarot cards differs not one whit from any of the other mystical pretenses to fortune-telling or personality analysis.

Tarot has not been scientifically validated as having any importance in matters of reality.

Regular playing cards or dominoes can be used for "fortune-telling."

Other claims to fortune telling and mystical personality analysis are also devoid of scientific substance.

Many, probably most, practitioners of each category are sincere. Many are perceptive, sensitive people with vivid imaginations. A minority are frauds. At the legal level, whether they are frauds or sincere makes all the difference in the world. It is also of some academic interest. However, regarding your decision as to whether to live your life following these mystics, their sincerity, self-deception, or criminal intent should not be the basis for your decision. Your first point of decision should rest solely on whether the claimed craft has any validity. If it does not—and it does not—then don't get taken!

In prior chapters we analyzed in detail several mystical claims. You now know how they work, or, more precisely, how they do not work. Rather than dwell at length on each of the other bits of nonsense masquerading as science, suffice it to say that none of the following has been scientifically validated. Not one of them is worth your time, energy, or money. Following, in no particular order, are other claimed methods of fortune telling, claimed methods of personality analysis, as well as other claimed mystical forces and phenomena.

Remote viewing (also known as an out-of-body experience; another alias is astral projection) is the purported ability to transport one's spirit, soul, mind, or awareness out of the body to view things and events at another place. In spite of many claims, there has been no proof under good, careful, scientifically controlled conditions that the phenomenon exists at all.

"FAX MACHINE RECEIVES PHOTO FROM HEAVEN." Thus read the banner headline in the March 7, 1989, issue of the *Sun*, a tabloid sold at the checkout counters of many supermarkets and stores. Accompanying a picture of a chimpanzee and a little boy, on that same cover, was the article "BOY AND CHIMP ARE BROTHER AND SISTER." In case you want more excitement, that very same front page also featured an article "Magic wallet turns play money into real cash." The paper sells, so we must conclude that at least some people believe those extraordinary claims.

People pretend to tell your fortune by throwing and interpreting various things: dice, runes, *I-ching*, and more.

Crystal-ball gazing is another claimed method of telling you all about you, as well as a claimed pipeline to peek into your future—for a fee, of course.

Reincarnation is making a comeback. Oh, by the way, I was a Russian serf in my previous life. I have met numerous people who claim to have been kings, queens, knights, pirates, and assorted other swashbucklers in their previous lives. I have never met anyone claiming to have been a Russian serf. There were far more Russian serfs than any other category named above. Ergo, by statistical deduction, I must have been a Russian serf. No, of course I do not believe that. Do you?

Alchemists are from bygone days. It was claimed and believed that they could change base metals into valuable metals, for example, lead into gold. Rubbish.

Rainmakers have also passed from the current scene.

Clairvoyance, extrasensory perception (ESP), and telepathy are claimed methods of communication which defy the known laws of nature. They are outside the realm of science. I do not wish to pass over these items too lightly or too hastily. There is much written about them, and many people believe in them. Bay Area Skeptics, an organization which I helped found and for which I was the first Chair, has had for many years a standing offer of $11,000 for anyone who can demonstrate these abilities under properly controlled scientific conditions. If you are in the San Francisco Bay Area and believe that you have these "gifts," or know someone else who does, do please contact me. I have given presentations at universities where I have convinced a substantial portion of the audience that I have these miraculous powers. We stand ready to test you.

Psychokinesis, also known as telekinesis, is the claimed ability to move objects at a distance. No one has demonstrated that with proper controls.

Channeling is simply spiritualism recycled. The claim is that the mystic can contact the dead. The dead supposedly speak through the mystical reader.

Water dowsers (also known as water witches) claim to be able to find underground water by walking across the land holding two sticks. The sticks dip down over the sight of the water, or so we are told. Geologists can do that, too. And so can many lay people. The scientific testing of water dowsers has shown that they are not able to find water any better than random expectation.

Biorhythms are the claimed three cycles that follow you through life: the physical cycle has 23 days, the emotional cycle has 28 days, and the intellectual cycle has 33 days. They start on the day of your birth, and are claimed to be immutable throughout your entire life, regardless of traumas, illnesses, accidents, or statistics which conclusively prove the opposite conclusions.

The Bermuda Triangle, also known as The Devil's Triangle, is a section of the North Atlantic Ocean bounded by Bermuda, Puerto Rico, and Melbourne, Florida. It is claimed that an inordinate number of ships and planes mysteriously disappear in this area. I was challenged to explain this while appearing as a guest on a radio talk show. A caller demanded that I explain why the commercial airlines never fly over the Bermuda Triangle, if it is all bunkum, as I had claimed.

When the hourly news broadcast interrupted our interview, I had the opportunity to make a few telephone calls. I was then able to make an important point: before you attempt to determine and explain *why* something happens, it is important to ascertain *whether* the claimed phenomenon happens. My telephone calls to three commercial airlines elicited the information that all three of them do in fact regularly fly over the area known as The Bermuda Triangle. Tracking and tracing the stories, we learn that many of the claimed disappearances are easily explained, many of the stories are erroneous, some of the ships were in fact sunk well outside of the Bermuda Triangle, and many facts are in error, exaggerated, or simply flat-out wrong. For the full treatment on this, for a competent, scientific investigation, I happily refer you to *The Bermuda Triangle Mystery Solved* (Kusche 1975).

Mystical healers and forecasters, such as Edgar Cayce and Nostradamus, have not been validated. Their errors, misses, and vagueness allow them to be totally discounted.

"Pyramid Power" and "Crystal Power" are figments of the imaginations of many people.

Palmistry, reading of tea leaves or coffee grounds, graphology, phrenology (reading of bumps on the head), and numerology are more of the same.

Other: Having now inserted the category "Other," no one can ever accuse me of omitting any. The list goes on.

At a party, someone who was impressed with my reading of the tarot cards inquired, "Can you also read palms?"

Forgive me, dear reader, but I think that my answer, albeit a bit crude, will serve to make a point: "I have studied the craft of cold reading and am skilled in the art. With equal grace and confidence, I can read buffalo shit."

PART III

CONS, SWINDLES, SCAMS, AND OTHER DIVERSIONS

Chapter 10

The Pigeon Drop

The . . . old-time con techniques . . . have changed very little over the years. No matter how often these cons are used and how much publicity they receive, they never seem to go out of style; people continue to fall for them.
Money for Nothing (Henderson 1986, 42).

My investigations and research lead me to conclude that the Pigeon Drop is the all-time favorite con game. It is quick, lucrative, and, alas, has a low record of apprehension and conviction of the criminals.

For a variety of reasons, senior citizens are most vulnerable to this con, and are therefore the favorite marks sought by the grifters. Senior citizens tend to be available, often live alone, have the time and inclination to talk to strangers, and tend to be trusting and often obedient. Although frequently living on a fixed income, many have their life savings readily available in a savings account or certificate of deposit.

There are many variations on the theme. We will take
you through one scene. Please be aware that the cons who
approach you may take a different tack.

You are lonely. You went for a morning walk in the park.
Now you are resting on a park bench. Children are playing
baseball in the distance. Squirrels and birds are foraging for
food in the grass. You long for someone to talk to, for
someone to take an interest in you.

"Lovely day, isn't it? Mind if I sit here for a while?" An
attractive, well-dressed woman in her early fifties is standing at the other end of the bench. At her question, of course
you invite her to sit down.

In a little while, you are talking as if you were old friends
who had known each other for years. You have learned a
lot about her: her name is Jane; she is a widow, lonely, a
retired schoolteacher, and is pleased to have the opportunity
to speak with you. And she has learned a lot about you. You
really opened up. You told her all about how your children
have married and moved away, how you live alone, and you
admit that you too are lonely. Without sensing that there
was any problem, you even told her where you keep your
savings account—just down the street.

The time is passing delightfully. Then a young, brash
woman, early twenties, whose dress and demeanor can be
described as scuzzy, interrupts your conversation, "Either
of you lose this satchel?"

The young woman is holding a leather pouch. You and
Jane both volunteer that it is not yours.

The young woman inquires, "What should we do with
it?"

Jane asks, "What's in it?"

The young woman does not know. Jane suggests that
you open it.

Upon opening the pouch, you discover a big wad of
hundred dollar bills. You watch as they count it: $12,000!

A serious discussion ensues to determine what should be done with the find. Oops! There is a note inside. The handwritten note reads: "Bill, this is your half of the money we won gambling. Remember, we are not going to report this to Internal Revenue Service. Not a word to anyone!"

You suggest turning it over to the police. The young woman protests, "No way! They'll just keep the money."

The sassy manner of the young woman upsets you. You look to Jane for some quiet reassurance about the entire transaction.

Jane calmly observes, "Well, I don't think the police would keep it," hastily adding, "but you never know. Besides, since it is gambling money, the loss probably will not be reported to the police.

"What should we do?" you inquire.

Jane has a ready answer, "My lawyer's office is just a few doors away. Let me go ask him. You two wait here."

Jane leaves, while you and the young woman remain with the money. You feel a great deal of stress, and look off into the distance, concentrating on the children's baseball game.

Jane returns to announce, "My lawyer agrees that we should not turn it in to the police. I told him about the note, and he said it was unlikely that the owner would come in to claim it. However, he told me there is a state law which requires us to hold on to the money for 30 days. After that we can split it."

You are getting more excited. One-third of $12,000 is $4,000.

Jane continues, "He said that he could hold it in his safe. He said that each of us should put up $2,500 in good faith money."

You balk, "Why do we have to put up any money?"

Jane replies, "Well, that's what my lawyer said. He explained that there has to be some assurance that we are reliable."

The young woman blurts out, "Hey, I'll be able to scrounge up the $2,500 for my share. Hell, in 30 days I'll get back my $2,500 plus $4,000 more!"

Jane assures you that she will put up her $2,500.

You balk once more.

The young woman gets very angry, turns to Jane and points to you as she speaks, "Hey, the hell with that one." Then, addressing Jane, she continues, "You and I can split this two ways. We don't need a third person. That way we'll each get $6,000. Besides, I'm the one who found the money. I don't need either of you." She quickly modifies that, again speaking to Jane, "Well, I do need you. After all, it was your lawyer who advised us what to do."

You feel that you may have said something wrong. You feel your $4,000 slipping away.

Jane tries to calm the young woman, "Please try to understand. We are all a little excited." She then turns toward you, "Come on, you were with us when we found the money. You are entitled to share in it."

Now, dear reader, you are at the moment of decision. Do you let the $4,000 slip away? Or do you go along with it?

To complete our story, let us assume that you go along. Jane walks you to your bank to withdraw your $2,500 good faith money. You have agreed that you will all meet back at the park bench in twenty minutes.

On the way to the bank, Jane explains that she did not think ahead. Her bank is an hour's drive away. With the round trip plus stopping in the bank, she probably could not return for about two and a half hours.

You are now all caught up in the excitement of what is going on. You do not wish to delay it, and express that to Jane.

Jane inquires if you know where she can cash a check.

You volunteer to endorse her check, and she can cash it at your savings bank.

You enter the bank, withdraw $2,500, and endorse Jane's check for $2,500. She then cashes it.

On your return to the park bench, you discover that the young woman is already there waiting for you.

You and the young woman hand over your money to Jane. Jane leaves to go to her lawyer's office with $19,500 in cash: the $12,000 that was found plus $2,500 good faith money from each of the three of you.

When Jane returns, she informs you that her attorney friend would like to talk to you. You feel some relief at this. Much as you trusted Jane, you were a bit uneasy. You like that idea that you will talk to the lawyer. Jane gives you the name, address and suite number. It is just down the block.

You leave Jane and the young woman at the bench, while you go to see the lawyer.

It is over! You have been taken! You discover that there is no such attorney in the building. Upon your return to the park bench, Jane and friend are long gone. Your money is long gone.

How much did this cost you? If you said $2,500, you are wrong. Surely you do not think that "Jane's" check will be honored. That will be dishonored, as being drawn against insufficient funds, or the check may have been stolen, or there may be no such bank account—the check may be a counterfeit. In any event, I assure you that it will not be honored. You lost $5,000 in about half an hour!

Notice how early in the game they introduced the word "we." They immediately involved you in the proceedings.

By the way, did you really watch the count of the money closely? In reality, there may have been only one or two hundred dollar bills on the outside; inside there were one-dollar bills or even play money. You were not really watching.

You did not count the young woman's $2,500 either. She may not have had that much. All you are really sure of is that $5,000 went with "Jane." That is the $5,000 that came out of your savings account.

There is *never* a reason for you to withdraw cash from your bank account to prove anything to anyone. There is *never* a reason for you to put up cash as "good faith" money. There is *never* an urgency for you go to your bank to take out large amounts of cash in order to turn it over to a stranger. There is *never* a legitimate deal which requires immediate cash given to a stranger. There is *never* a reason for you to endorse a check to be cashed by a total stranger. There is *never* a reason to enter a shady deal. There is *never* a reason to be afraid to report a legitimate deal to the police.

Chapter 11

The Bank
Examiner Scam

No federal, state, or local law enforcement agency, or any bank official, would ever request that a customer withdraw money to participate in an internal investigation.
Bank of America (1987, Oct. p. 2).

You are sitting home, quietly reading the morning paper, when the telephone rings.

"Good morning, Mrs. Orange. This is William G. Blue. I am a bank examiner with the Federal Bureau of Investigation. We suspect a teller in your bank has been embezzling money from customers' accounts. By the way, Mrs. Orange, which branch do you bank at?"

You tell him.

"Ah, yes, the West Branch of the, uh, the. . . ."

Being courteous, and trying to save him any embarrassment, you tell him the name of your bank.

"Oh, yes, of course, it says it right here in my files. We would like your cooperation in our investigation. We would like you to withdraw $3,000 in cash from your bank account. The serial numbers on the money have already been noted.

"After you get the money, we'll meet you outside of the bank to take the money. I will personally pick it up. I'll take the money to my office to compare the serial numbers with our list. After that, we'll return to the bank and deposit the money back into your account. It will be back in your account by the end of the day. The bank president is cooperating in our investigation. He has assured me that you will not lose any interest on the account during the brief time the money is out, and furthermore that he will honor any checks drawn against that amount. He can do this because he knows the money will be out only long enough for us to check the serial numbers. The total time will be only about two hours.

"Oh, one final word, Mrs. Orange: In order to maintain strict audit control on this investigation, it is essential that you mention this to no one. Not even your husband. . . . Oh, I am truly sorry. I didn't know that you were a widow.

"Thank you so much for your cooperation. The bank president has informed me that you will have your picture in the local newspaper with him and the mayor of the town. All of us appreciate your cooperation and your recognition of your civic duty. This town is lucky to have upright citizens such as you."

You draw out the money, as instructed. When you leave the bank, a well-dressed gentleman meets you. He identifies himself as Mr. Blue. You hand him the money. He instructs you to leave the area, and not to return to the bank until at least the next day.

That is the last you hear, until you receive your bank statement at the end of the month. At that time, you learn that your $3,000 is gone. Or perhaps you will find out earlier, when your bank informs you that some of your checks have bounced. You have insufficient funds in your account to cover them.

Notice that, at the time of the call, "Mr. Blue" did not know the name of your bank. He tricked you into telling him by starting with the branch, and then by appearing to stumble over the name of the bank. In some cases, the con artist may have found out from some other source where you bank.

The end of this chapter is the same as the beginning. Please reread the quote at the top of this chapter.

Chapter 12

Pyramid Schemes

This get-rich scheme is a scam. There is no Santa Claus, Tooth Fairy or free lunch. Chain letters requesting money are illegal. I am sending this "business opportunity" offer to the postmaster, which is what every person should do when a letter of this kind shows up in the mail.
    Dear Abby column, June 6, 1988 (Van Buren 1988).

The response in the *Dear Abby* column specifically addresses the pyramid scheme analyzed in this chapter. We shall explore it in depth.

You may merely scan the mathematics at the end of the chapter. You need not analyze every statistic.

It was necessary for me to go through the exercise in order to be able to assure you of the following: The pyramid scheme analyzed is more than illegal, and it is more than a bad investment. It is even more than a fraud. The scheme cannot possibly work. The person who started it knowingly, willfully, and maliciously lied. That lie was done for the sole purpose of fraudulently obtaining money.

On April 12, 1989, I received the following letter:
Hello:

My name is Joe Strelecki. In September 1985, my car was repossessed and bill collectors were hounding me like you would not believe. I was laid off and my unemployment had run out. In January, 1986, my family and I went on a 10 day cruise. In February I bought a new Cadillac with cash. I am now building a home in Virginia and will never have to work again. All because in October of 1985 I received a letter in the mail telling me how I can earn $50,000 any time I wanted to. Of course I was skeptical and even a little angry that anyone would think me so gullible, but because I was desperate and had nothing to lose, I tried it.

TODAY I AM RICH!

I have made over $200,000 to date, and I will become a millionaire within the next year. This money program works perfectly every time. I have never failed to make at least $50,000 each time. This is a legitimate business opportunity, a perfectly legal money making program which does not require you to sell anything or come in contact with anyone, best of all you only have to leave home to mail these letters.

If you would like that Lucky Break that everyone searches for, follow these instructions carefully and in 20 to 60 days you will have made $50,000 in cash.

1. Immediately mail $1.00 to each of the five names listed below. CASH ONLY. Wrap in plain white paper.

2. Remove the name in number 1 spot, move the other names up one, and put your name in the number 5 position.

3. Xerox or print 100 copies with your name in the number 5 position.

4. Get a list of 100 names from S. E. Ring Mailing Lists. Address: P. O. Box 15061, Fort Lauderdale, FL 33318. Cost $13.00 per 100 names.

5. While you are waiting for your mailing list to arrive, place your letters in envelopes and put stamps on them. DO NOT PLACE YOUR RETURN ADDRESS ON THEM.

6. When your list arrives, it will be on the pre glued labels. Simply stick the labels on your envelopes and mail them. Within 60 days, you will have received $50,000 in cash. THIS IS LEGAL!

FOLLOW THESE INSTRUCTIONS TO GET ON THE ROAD TO RICHES! ! ! !

The above is followed by a list of the names and addresses of five persons; "Joe Strelecki" was not one of them.

For the purpose of analyzing this, let us assume that "Joe Strelecki" really exists and is telling the complete truth.

According to his testimony, when he received the letter in October 1985, it was already in the works. He has represented that he has worked it through many cycles.

Rather than trace it through many cycles, we shall trace it through one cycle only. Let us see where the figures lead.

To reduce our computations to a rock-bottom minimum, let us assume that "Strelecki" received it right near the beginning. Since he made no mention that he was an originator, we must assume that he received the letter as I did: with five names already on it. Therefore, at minimum, he started his processing in Step 6.

At this point, please refer to the tabulations at the end of this chapter. After doing that, please come back to read the remaining text.

One final note. On July 9, 1988, I received a letter which began:

> Hi, my name is Dave Rhodes. In Sept 1983 my car was repossessed and bill collectors were hounding me. I was laid off and my unemployment had run out. In Jan 1984, my family and I went on a 10 day cruise. In Feb 1984, I bought a 1984 Cadillac for cash. I am currently building a home in Virginia and I'll never have to work again. In Oct 1983, I received a letter in the mail telling me how I could earn $50,000 or more whenever I wanted. I was very skeptical but decided to try it because I was desperate and had nothing to lose. I scraped together the few dollars needed and got started. Today I am rich! I have earned over $200,000 to date and will become a millionaire within the next 4 to 6 months. Anyone, believe me, can do the same. This money making program works perfectly every time, 100%.

He mentions that he earns at least $50,000 each time, and goes on to assure me:

> This is a legitimate business opportunity—a perfectly legal money making program. . . . YOUR DREAMS WILL COME TRUE.

This pyramid scheme, as are all pyramid schemes, is a con game. It is illegal. You can be prosecuted criminally if your participate.

Furthermore, it is an extraordinarily poor investment. You cannot win.

I trust that I have presented sufficient information for you to conclude that, while participation may land you in jail, this illegal scam will not and cannot make your dreams come true.

THE POSTAL PYRAMID SCHEME OF "JOE STRELECKI":
TABULATIONS

STEP #

1   Originator mails it to 100 people.

2   All recipients process it. Each mails it to 100 people. Plus, each mails $1 to the one name on the list.

3   All recipients process it. Each mails it to 100 people. Plus, each mails $1 to each of the two names on the list.

4   All recipients process it. Each mails it to 100 people. Plus, each mails $1 to each of the three names on the list.

5   All recipients process it. Each mails it to 100 people. Plus, each mails $1 to each of the four names on the list. One of the recipients is "Joe Strelecki."

6   All recipients process it. Each mails it to 100 people. Plus, each mails $1 to each of the five names on the list. "Strelecki" starts his processing at this step. He is number 5 on the list he mails out.

7   All recipients process it. Each mails it to 100 people. Plus, each mails $1 to each of the five names on the list. "Strelecki" is number 4 on the list mailed out.

8   All recipients process it. Each mails it to 100 people. Plus, each mails $1 to each of the five names on the list. "Strelecki" is number 3 on the list mailed out.

9   All recipients process it. Each mails it to 100 people. Plus, each mails $1 to each of the five names on the list. "Strelecki" is number 2 on the list mailed out.

10 All recipients process it. Each mails it to 100 people. Plus, each mails $1 to each of the five names on the list. "Strelecki" is number 1 on the list mailed out.

11 All recipients process it. Each mails it to 100 people. Plus, each mails $1 to each of the five names on the list. "Strelecki" cashes in on this mailing. He is off the list. You are finally one of the recipients!

12 All recipients process it. Each mails it to 100 people. Plus, each mails $1 to each of the five names on the list. You start your processing at this step. You are number 5 on the list you mail out.

13 All recipients process it. Each mails it to 100 people. Plus, each mails $1 to each of the five names on the list. You are number 4 on the list mailed out.

14 All recipients process it. Each mails it to 100 people. Plus, each mails $1 to each of the five names on the list. You are number 3 on the list mailed out.

15 All recipients process it. Each mails it to 100 people. Plus, each mails $1 to each of the five names on the list. You are number 2 on the list mailed out.

16 All recipients process it. Each mails it to 100 people. Plus, each mails $1 to each of the five names on the list. You are number 1 on the list mailed out. You are at the top of the list!

17 All recipients process it. Each mails it to 100 people. Plus, each mails $1 to each of the five names on the list. This is your final cashing in. You have cashed in and are out!

Now let us look at some figures (see page over).

The first figure in each step is the mailing of letters. The second figure is the dollar amount sent in that mailing.

Number of Mailings for This Process

Step #
1 100
2 10,000
  100
3 1,000,000
 20,000
4 100,000,000
  3,000,000
5 10,000,000,000
  400,000,000
6 1,000,000,000,000
  50,000,000,000
7 100,000,000,000,000
 5,000,000,000,000
8 10,000,000,000,000,000
 500,000,000,000,000
9 1,000,000,000,000,000,000
  50,000,000,000,000,000
10 100,000,000,000,000,000,000
  5,000,000,000,000,000,000
11 10,000,000,000,000,000,000,000
  500,000,000,000,000,000,000
12 1,000,000,000,000,000,000,000,000
  50,000,000,000,000,000,000,000
13 100,000,000,000,000,000,000,000,000
 5,000,000,000,000,000,000,000,000
14 10,000,000,000,000,000,000,000,000,000
 500,000,000,000,000,000,000,000,000
15 1,000,000,000,000,000,000,000,000,000,000
  50,000,000,000,000,000,000,000,000,000
16 100,000,000,000,000,000,000,000,000,000,000
  5,000,000,000,000,000,000,000,000,000,000
17 10,000,000,000,000,000,000,000,000,000,000,000
  500,000,000,000,000,000,000,000,000,000,000

Total: 10,606,060,606,060,606,060,606,060,504,030,200

The previous chart only considers each individual mailing. This chart accumulates the mailings.

Cumulative mailings

1	 100
2	10,100
	10,200
3	 1,010,200
	 1,030,200
4	 101,030,200
	 104,030,200
5	 10,104,030,200
	 10,504,030,200
6	 1,010,504,030,200
	 1,060,504,030,200
7	 101,060,504,030,200
	 106,060,504,030,200
8	10,106,060,504,030,200
	10,606,060,504,030,200
9	 1,010,606,060,504,030,200
	 1,060,606,060,504,030,200
10	 101,060,606,060,504,030,200
	 106,060,606,060,504,030,200
11	 10,106,060,606,060,504,030,200
	 10,606,060,606,060,504,030,200
12	 1,010,606,060,606,060,504,030,200
	 1,060,606,060,606,060,504,030,200
13	 101,060,606,060,606,060,504,030,200
	 106,060,606,060,606,060,504,030,200
14	10,106,060,606,060,606,060,504,030,200
	10,606,060,606,060,606,060,504,030,200
15	 1,010,606,060,606,060,606,060,504,030,200
	 1,060,606,060,606,060,606,060,504,030,200
16	 101,060,606,060,606,060,606,060,504,030,200
	 106,060,606,060,606,060,606,060,504,030,200
17	 10,106,060,606,060,606,060,606,060,504,030,200
	 10,606,060,606,060,606,060,606,060,504,030,200

Estimated Population of the World - 1985:

4,882,000,000 (*Tribune* 1988, 522).

Number of mailings each person in the world would have to make in order to make his claim true:

2,172,482,713,244,700,000,000,000.

That is, every man, woman, and child on earth would have to mail more than 2 septillion letters for one cycle.

It might make it easier on you if I were to say more than 2 trillion trillion letters.

He claims that in 20 to 60 days, you will complete the cycle. That means that the maximum time for one process, once you mail it out, is 60 days. You started the process at step 12, and were out after step 17. Total mailings during that 60-day period:

10,606,060,606,050,000,000,000,000,000,000,000.

Let us continue:

For each man, woman, and child on earth during that 60-day period, that would require:

Number of letters required to be mailed by each person during that 60-day period:

2,172,482,713,242,520,000,000,000.

Number of letters required to be mailed by each person every single day:

36,208,045,220,709,000,000,000.

Assuming an 8-hour workday, number of letters required to be mailed by each person every single hour:

4,526,005,652,589,000,000,000.

Number of letters required to be mailed by each person every single minute:

75,433,427,543,000,000,000.

Number of letters required to be mailed by each person every single second:

1,257,223,792,000,000,000.

You would have to work a solid 8-hour day, every single day, for 60 days in a row. You would have to be productive every second, mailing out more than 1 quintillion letters every second.

Before closing, let us review the additional information that would have to be taken into account in order to make the above computations more accurate: We computed the processing per person by dividing the total processings by the estimated number of persons in the world. We must assume that some people are too young to process their share: for example, a one-day-old baby.

We must further assume that some people are too infirm to process their share: for example, someone in a coma. We must also assume that at least some people would be too busy with other things to process their share. Therefore, the workers would have to pick up that slack, adding to their processing of more than 1 quintillion letters per second.

Furthermore, there are other factors to consider: The letter would have to be translated into all of the languages of the earth. The money would have to be converted into all of the currencies of the earth. At each mailing, there would have to be money mailed out. Starting with Step 6, each processing would require a mailing of $5 by each person.

For Step 17 alone, this would mean a mailing of:
$500,000,000,000,000,000,000,000,000,000,000.
That is $500 nonillion.

To get some understanding of the meaning of $500 nonillion, if you were to spend $1,000,000 every *second* of every minute of every hour of every day in the year, it would take you over 150 million billion *centuries* to spend $500 nonillion.

For just one cycle, at $.25 per mailing, postage alone would cost:
$2,651,515,151,515,150,000,000,000,000,000.
That figure does not consider costs of paper and envelopes.

And lastly, please remember that we computed the above for one single cycle only, in order to put you through it just once. Mr. "Joe Strelecki" claims that it has operated for many cycles over the course of several years. I received his letter a full three years after he had allegedly first cashed in on this wonder. It was still being circulated. In order to compute what effort went into that, you need simply multiply the above figures by whatever number of cycles you wish to imagine.

Now please return to the text.

Chapter 13

Three-Card Monte and Other Gambling Scams

Think of a con game as a play—with actors and actresses, a plot, a well-rehearsed script and even a stage of sorts (on the street outside a bank lobby, for example, or at the victim's home). Although the victim doesn't know it at the time, he or she is part of the cast. The acting often is superb, the stage setting just right, the performance flawless. Curtain.

Sting Shift: The Street-Smart Cop's Handbook of Cons and Swindles (Smith & Walstad 1989, 9).

If you walk along the streets of any major city in the world, you are likely to run across some street scams in progress. One of the favorites is the three-card monte. It can be set up quickly, using boxes, a smooth rock, a wide railing, or any of a hundred other surfaces. It uses only three playing cards. When the police are spotted, it can be folded up in three seconds, and the cons can disperse among the crowd.

The operator shows you three ordinary playing cards: two of one color and one of another. For example, it might be two red aces and a black ace, or two red aces and a black queen, or two red queens and a black queen. The use of the queens has earned it the name, in some circles, "broad-tossing" or "tossing the broads."

The cards are bent lengthwise by folding the face inward. This makes it easy to pick them up from a flat surface.

"All right, are you ready to play? Not yet. That's fine, friend. You are welcome to watch."

The operator shows the three cards to you. Let us use aces for this example. He has a red ace in his left hand and a red ace in his right hand. Now he picks up the black ace with his left hand—it is underneath the red ace. He faces it toward you, so that you can see it clearly.

The black ace is put down on the table, then it is picked up by the right hand. Again, the cards are shown to you. All the while, the red aces are still held in his hands.

He does this a few more times, then lays down all of the cards. "Do you want to bet where the black ace is? No?" The lady standing on your left puts down $20 on the card on your left. The operator turns over the card she bet on; it is the black ace. He pays her back her $20 plus an additional $20.

Hmmmmmmm. It looks easy. You knew it was that card. You decide to watch once more.

Again he goes through this simple procedure. This time, the gentleman standing on your right puts $30 on the middle card. It is turned over; the gentleman wins. He picks up his $30 plus an additional $30. Again you knew. You could have won.

You watch it a few more times. It is easy to the point of being silly.

You take your wallet out of your pocket/purse. You think you detect a faint smile on the face of the operator, but you are not sure.

Again the cards are tossed. When they come down, you are sure you saw the black ace come down in the center. As you think about that, both the lady and the gentleman bet on the center card: she puts down $40, and he bets $50. Taking courage from this, you put down $30.

Oops! You missed. The black ace is on your left. You just lost $30. You must have not paid attention. You will win it back next time.

I'll spare you the agony of the next several minutes. You lose every time. The lady wins sometimes; the gentleman wins sometimes; you never win. Have you figured out why?

The "lady" and the "gentleman" are con artists. They are *shills*, working with the operator. A shill pretends to be the same position that you are, or sometimes pretends to be on your side, working with you. In fact, the shill is a secret accomplice of the operator.

You assumed that they were betting against the operator, just as you were. In fact, you have walked into a well-rehearsed play. You get the Academy Award as the sucker.

Allow me to assure you that you will *never* win at this game. After the cards come down, when showing them to you, they can make a switch. Unless you are trained and experienced in gambling or magic, you will not see it. Even if you *know* where the card is, I promise you that you will not win.

My friend Jack was sure he knew the game well enough to beat the street operators. I tried to warn him against playing, but he would not listen.

When the cards came down, he slammed his hand down on the card on his left and proclaimed, "I'll bet $20 on that card!" With his certainty that he had followed the action, and with his hand resting firmly on the card, to prevent a switch, he was secure that he would win.

The operator, without batting an eyelash, paid off the man standing next to Jack. Jack protested, "I won! Pay me!" The operator replied, "If you won, why would I have paid him off?"

The logic of the operator left much to be desired. Jack argued some more. It was obvious (to me) that the man who had been paid off was a shill. The operator answered with, "Look, buddy, I'll let you take your $20 back." Jack claimed that he had won and was entitled to another $20. Suddenly two gigantic men appeared from the shadows and began to close in. As Jack began to speak, one of the newcomers put his massive hand on Jack's shoulder and said quietly, but authoritatively, "Sir, I am sure that you would not want to make any trouble." A bulky hand suddenly landed on Jack's other shoulder, as the other giant spoke quietly, "I am sure, too."

There you have it, folks. They will not pay off. Just move on.

✳ ✳ ✳ ✳ ✳

With all of my experience in studying these games, I still meet with surprises. A friend, let's call him David, had invited me to join him for breakfast. He brought along his friend John.

At introduction time, David told John that I am a magician. John was interested in that, and inquired what type of work I do. This was some years ago, just before my first presentation to the California Crime Prevention Officers Association. I told David and John that I was making a major study of gambling scams, since I would be making a presentation to the police in a few weeks. John pumped me for more information.

I took a deck of cards from my pocket. I shuffled and cut it, then dealt draw poker to John and me. John was looking at four kings and an ace. I had three jacks. In showing my hand to David, I "accidentally" flashed it so that John could see it. I "of course" did not know that John had seen my hand.

I inquired how many cards John wanted to draw. He confidently assured me that he would stand pat. I said I wanted two cards. Cleanly and slowly, I discarded two cards and took two cards off the top of the pack.

I asked John what he wanted to bet. Immediately and enthusiastically he replied, "Two hundred dollars." Assuming, *in error*, that he was in play mode, I replied, "All right, two hundred dollars play money."

John hastily assured me, "No, really!"

In disbelief, I uttered an astonished, "What?"

John made it clear, "I really want to bet two hundred dollars on this hand!"

Still reeling, I replied, "You've got to be kidding!"

John truly wanted to bet two hundred dollars on the hand. It was the classic con set-up: He had seen the deck shuffled and cut. He obviously has no idea what magicians are capable of doing. He was looking at four kings and an ace. He had illegally peeked at my hand. He saw that I had three jacks. He saw me cleanly discard two cards and take two cards. The best I could have was four jacks, right? Wrong! I had a straight flush!

He sweated a bit. I could not and would not take his $200, even though he was ready, willing, and champing at the bit to take $200 of my money. Some friends have told me that he deserved to lose, and that I should have taken his money.

That was one of the times that I truly understood what drives some con artists to their rationalization: He would have gladly taken my money, by cheating; why should I not take his?

What John did was outrageous from two points of view. First, he knew I was a magician who was studying gambling scams. It is a mistake to try to beat someone at his/her own game. Second, it was a friendly breakfast. It was grotesque that he was anxious to cheat me out of $200.

✳ ✳ ✳ ✳ ✳ ✳

At a dinner party, a young man attempted to pull a triple coup: to impress the family of his fiancee with his wealth and his shrewdness, to show that he could con the magician, and to win $100 in the bargain.

Our budding young con artist pulled out a crisp, new one-hundred dollar bill and laid it on the table. On top of it he placed an empty wine glass. On the lip of the wine glass he balanced two pennies, on opposite sides. He confidently looked me in the eye and boldly challenged, "I'll bet you that hundred dollars that you can't pull the bill out without spilling the pennies. You can't touch either the glass or the pennies; you can only touch the bill."

It would have been inappropriate for me to win $100 from him. All roads lead to that: my conscience, my ethics, my morals, and my solemn oath pledged to The Society of American Magicians, as well as to other magic organizations to which I belong. I calmly replied, "Save your money."

Not one to give up easily, he pursued the challenge, repeatedly hurling down the gauntlet, to the point of being abusive and insulting. Again and again I tried to parry, but he would not let go. When he finally got around to calling me a phony, a chicken, and to telling everyone that I was bluffing, I informed him, "I'll tell you what. I will give you a free lesson. There is no bet riding on this." Then I slowly rolled up the one-hundred dollar bill toward the glass. As it rolled in, the bill slid out from under the glass. The pennies stayed nicely balanced on the lip of the glass.

Handing back his hundred-dollar bill, I said, "Here is your bill back. You just saved $100."

Instantly he replied, "Most people don't know that."

"I am not most people," I assured him.

He still would not let go, continuing with, "Most people try to pull the bill out quickly. That always spills the pennies."

"Save your money," I quietly intoned.

He was again ready for the challenge. He ostentatiously pulled out another crisp, new one-hundred dollar bill. Again he prepared the set-up with the bill, the glass, and the two pennies. Then he confidently proclaimed, "I'll bet you that hundred-dollar bill that you can't pull out the bill without rolling it up, without touching the glass or the pennies, and without spilling the pennies."

Again I tried to tell him to save his money.

He pushed and baited and insulted again. Finally I had enough. I calmly, well, reasonably calmly, stated, "I'll tell you what. I will give you another free lesson. There is no bet riding on this."

I grabbed the sides of the hundred-dollar bill, with one hand on each side. Then I paused for a moment: Yes, I confess, there is a bit of theater in me. You indeed could have heard a pin drop, as every eye at the dinner party was fixed on my hands, the bill, the glass, and the pennies. Then, in one very sudden, swift movement, I yanked the bill out from under the glass. The glass stayed in place. The pennies jiggled a bit, but they did not fall.

Handing back his hundred-dollar bill, I said, "Here is your bill back. You have just saved $200. Do you have any other bets to propose?"

The young, defeated con artist was uncharacteristically quiet for the remainder of the evening.

I hope you people will understand, or at least forgive me for my behavior: I do not have a whole lot of sympathy for his type.

❋ ❋ ❋ ❋ ❋ ❋

There are more stories that I could tell. I could teach the methods for each of the games. Our purpose here is not to discuss how to beat the con artists at their own game. The grifters are not in business to lose. Do not try to beat them. Do not even think of trying to beat them.

Let us assume that you do not play the violin. Do you think you could read one book, study and plan for a week, and go on stage at Lincoln Center and perform playing the violin? Of course not.

How about performing brain surgery. Could you master that with one book and one week? Again, of course not.

The same goes for out-performing the professional football player.

Then do not think for one moment that you can read this book, study a bit, and be prepared to beat a professional, trained con artist at his/her rotten game. That is what those people do for a living. They have studied, practiced, and conned for years. With study and awareness, you will learn how to avoid them, and how to protect yourself and those you love. If you can learn that, if you can increase your chances to survive the attempts of the con artist, you and I will have accomplished our purpose in my writing and your reading this book.

Chapter 14

Carnival Games

There isn't a carnival game that I know of that hasn't been gaffed [fixed for the purpose of cheating] at one time or another. The same holds true for any casino game or private gambling game, be it dice, poker, gin rummy, Old Maid, or even tiddlywinks. They can all be gaffed.

All grifters must operate in more or less the same manner in order to fleece a player of a large sum of money. . . . I can give the reader one overall tip to prevent himself from being fleeced for a large sum. That is, whenever an operator of a game tells you he has a proposition for you, beware. If he permits you to wager a large sum of money on one spin of the wheel or one play at the game, it's a ten to one shot that the game is crooked. So, if you receive such a proposition from a game operator, don't walk away from the game—run.

The Amazing World of John Scarne (Scarne 1956, 122-123).

And what about the high striker? [You try to ring the bell by hitting the striker with a sledge hammer.]

That's one of the best crowd-pleasers in a carny. You get some skinny little kid or maybe a broad, and you let them ring the bell. And then some steel worker or gandy dancer [railroad worker] comes along, and you put on the brake and milk him for five or ten. If he's a big spender, you give him the cigar anyway. Hell, they only cost a nickel by the gross.

You see, the marker slides up along a track, like a railroad track, only smaller. The gaffer uses a squeeze device which pushes the two rails close together. Once he does that, nothing's going to ring that gong, no matter how hard it's hit.

   A Compendium of Bunk or How to Spot a Con Artist (Carey and Sherman 1976, 158).

Many of you may be surprised to find carnival games being discussed in a book that also deals with multimillion-dollar casino games, sophisticated card and dice cheating methods, and con games. The average person doesn't think of carnival games as even constituting gambling, let alone as a potential source of crooked gambling.

However, if you had ever seen, as I have, a wife pleading with her husband to leave a carnival game booth before he loses what little he has left of the week's living money, or another player so blinded by the desire to win that, after losing his money, he begs the game operator to accept his four-hundred-dollar camera as a wager on the game, or a victim sent home by a game agent to get a couple of hundred dollars to continue playing after he has been cheated out of all the cash he had on him, you might feel differently.

   Gambling Scams (Ortiz 1984, 157).

The unexpected news that a Carny has stepped from the sacred bond of silence has sent shock waves rippling through the industry. I am that Carny. . . . I am the one who has come forward to rip away the facade that is engulfing this bit of Americana and which is repeatedly making a mockery of clean sportsmanship and law and order—and pocketing millions of tax-free dollars in the process. I am committed to divulging every well-hidden secret, every illegal device that I know of now or learn of in the future.

   All About Carnivals (Sorrows 1985, 1-2).

Most carnival games can be played either straight or crooked (a two-way store). There is a good chance that just about any wheel-type game is going to be gaffed. Games that use point conversion charts are usually crooked (a razzle game). Any game where the operator looks at a number selected by a player could be run as a peek game.

   Sting Shift (Smith & Walstad, 1989, 92-93).

Crooked carnival games have been exposed in the past, but never to any great degree. . . . But here are the true facts laid bare, and the reader who has lost money to these parasites will learn how he lost it and why he should leave these games alone in the future. . . . If the reader gets pleasure out of losing his money on the games at carnivals, let him go ahead. There is more thrill to it than throwing cash in the gutter, but the net result to the average player is just the same. A fool and his money soon part on the carnival lot!
The Bunco Book (Gibson 1946, 22-24).

Nobody knows everything. I have made an extensive study of almost every topic covered in this book. That does not hold true for carnivals. From the time I was eleven years old (see Introduction), carnivals held no fascination for me. Although until recently I did not specifically know that I had been cheated, all my life I had an uneasy feeling that something was not right about my visit to the carnival. I was not drawn back to them until quite recently, and then only as an investigator, not as a player having fun.

Therefore, I have quoted experts—people who have done their homework in this field. I am saddened by the results.

Most of them hasten to point out, and I am sure that it is correct, that there are many honest, honorable operators of carnivals and carnival games. These writers, the honest operators, and I would like to see the criminal element weeded out.

If the games were honest, they would truly be fun. If they were fun, and if the people trusted them, more people would come to the carnivals. The operators of carnivals and carnival games would earn more money, and the general public would have more fun. It would be a win-win situation.

However, as for you, for now, you must deal with the situation as it is. Unless you are prepared to make an intensive study of the subject, I must tell you that you will have no way of knowing whether a particular carnival game is gaffed or honest. If you go, decide *in advance* how much you will spend for your fun, and stick to that amount. Do not go above it for any reason.

Chapter 15

Home Repair and Improvement Cons

If it ain't broke, don't fix it.
Anonymous.

Good afternoon, ma'am. I'm here to inspect your furnace."

You do not recall that anyone was supposed to come for that purpose. You inquire, "Who sent you?"

"Oh," he replies, "this is just a free inspection service."

"What do you do?" you ask. Notice that he did not answer your first question, and you have gone right by it. You allowed him to get away with his evasion. You must remain alert to such things.

"I do a free inspection of your furnace. Generally everything is all right. Even when there is a problem, it is usually quite small. In any event, before I leave, I will give you a written estimate and evaluation of the condition of your furnace."

"Well, all right." You agree to letting him in.

You hear him rattling around in the basement for about 20 minutes. Then he calls to you. He wants you to look at what he found. You go down into the basement. Fortunately, in our example, he is not a forcible robber or a rapist. But he could be. How could you allow yourself to get into such a position with a complete stranger who just walked up to your home and rang the doorbell?

Your furnace has been taken apart; parts are all over the floor. He informs you, "There are some serious problems here. I've drawn up this estimate. For $972, I can fix it and get it back into shipshape."

"But," you protest, "it was working fine. There was no hint of trouble."

He launches into an extensive explanation, using much technical language. You really do not understand a word that he says, but you conclude that it must be serious. You explain, "I will have to discuss this with my husband. Please put it back the way you found it."

"Ma'am," he replies, "didn't you understand my explanation? This is dangerous. If I put it back the way it was, it could explode."

Now you get scared. What do you do?

He continues, "I will be back on Thursday to put it back together. If you don't want the job that is really necessary, I can put it back with a new . . ." and he again goes into technical language which, to you, is gibberish. He concludes, "That will cost you only $197. It won't really solve your main problem, but it will at least protect you against the risk of explosion. That should get you through this winter."

By now you feel quite unsure and quite intimidated. You wish that you had waited on this whole thing. You ask him to please put it back the way it was. You promise to talk with your husband that evening, and that you will have an answer the next morning.

He balks, "Sorry, ma'am, but I can't put it back the way it was. I can't risk the lives of your entire family on a furnace that might explode."

You hastily ask, "Would it explode tonight?"

"I don't know, ma'am, but I sure ain't gonna take that risk with your life. I'm a professional."

You excuse yourself in order to telephone your husband at work. He is out on the road, and cannot be reached. You return to the "inspector." "I cannot reach my husband. I don't know what to do."

"Call me in the morning, ma'am."

You are now near panic: "But what about tonight? The temperature has been below zero outside at night. How will we survive the night without heat?"

He "explains" that you will survive better being a bit cold than you would if your furnace were to explode. He suggests that perhaps your family could stay with a neighbor.

Suddenly he "remembers" he has some used parts in his truck. He assures you that they are sturdy; he will guarantee them for three years. For just $135, he can put the furnace back together right away. With the parts he will install, he assures you that it will not explode. However, because he is not doing a complete job, and since the parts are used, he will have to insist on being paid in cash.

You are fully prepared to pay him that amount, have him put the furnace back together, and have him leave the house. You wish you had never met him. But, you do not have that much cash in the house, and you so inform him.

He asks how far away your bank is. It is about a 20-minute drive. He states, "Well, I will trust you. I'll start on the repairs. It will take about an hour, so you should easily be back from your bank by then."

Do you go and leave this stranger in your house? What do you do?

If you go to the bank, on your return you will find that he is gone, as are your silver, china, antiques, jewelry, your husband's golf clubs, and more. And your furnace will still be in pieces.

In the above story, if we had stopped the action at *any* point and asked what your proper action would have been, the answers would be: 1) Before you let him in: Do not let him in. Then call the police. 2) At *every* point after you let him in, the correct answer is: Call the police!

❊ ❊ ❊ ❊ ❊ ❊

A man selling smoke alarms came to my home some years ago. He offered to install the necessary smoke alarms for $800. (For the figures in this example, please make appropriate adjustments for inflation. This took place in the mid-1960s.) I told him I would like to think about it, and requested that he leave a brochure. He had no brochures. I requested a business card. He had none of those, either. I requested that he write his name and telephone number. He replied, "There's no point. Those who don't care enough about the lives of their families to sign up right away will never call back." I immediately shot back, "Well, of course not. You do not tell them how to reach you."

The next day I called a friend who was in the business and inquired about the price to set up my home with the necessary smoke alarms. He asked, "Who is buying lunch?" "I am," I replied. "$25."

The man who had walked in off the street had a contract ready for me to sign, but he did not have a brochure or even a business card. Would that have made you suspicious?

❊ ❊ ❊ ❊ ❊ ❊

"Excuse me, sir. We just completed a contracting job down the street. As we were riding by, we noticed several cracks in your driveway. We have some extra blacktop from the job we just did. If we take it back to the shop, we have to scrape it out of the truck, store it, and reload it for a future job. It would be cheaper for us to give you a real good price to blacktop your cracked driveway. Since we are already here and have this surplus material, we will do it for only $175. What do you say?"

If you say yes, you will most likely feel quite good about the deal you made . . . until the first rain. Then, all the oil, which you thought was high-grade blacktop, will be washed away.

✳ ✳ ✳ ✳ ✳ ✳

The guest on a radio talk show was very knowledgeable about real estate. His comments regarding investments, risks, financial analysis, appraisals, and other aspects of real estate were right on target. His answers to questions of those who called in were clearly based upon a good grounding in experience, education, and human nature.

Then came a question where he went off track.

A woman caller identified herself as a widow, in her sixties, who lived alone. She told the following story.

She had put an ad in the paper, asking for bids for an improvement to her home. She wanted to add a wing, so that her widowed daughter and grandchildren could live close by.

A man came to the house without calling first. She invited him in. He claimed to be a contractor. He spent about an hour and a half talking with her. As they spoke, he sketched plans. He quoted a price for the job.

Several days later, he called to inquire whether he got the job. She told him no. Then, according to her recounting of the story over the air, he told her that she owed him $50,000 for the work he had done preparing to complete the job. Relying upon her word, so he told her, he had purchased materials for the job.

She panicked. She quickly ended the conversation and got off the phone. She immediately telephone her daughter about the incident.

The next day, when the man called, the woman told him about her conversation with her daughter. The man said that he had filed a lien for $50,000 against the house.

At the conclusion of the conversation, the man telephoned the woman's daughter. He told her about the $50,000 lien on the house.

The radio caller was in tears by this point.

The real estate expert asked some incisive questions—to a point. Then, in my opinion, he dropped the ball.

He inquired if the caller had seen the papers for the lien. She had not. To short-cut the very painful exchange that followed, I will tell you that neither the caller nor her daughter had seen one piece of paper showing any lien on the house. Nor had there ever been a contract—the woman had not signed anything. Nor had the woman even orally heard about the alleged lien from anybody except the man demanding the $50,000.

At this point, the caller begged the real estate expert to advise her.

His first advice was that the caller's daughter should talk to the contractor again, in order to attempt to resolve it. If that did not solve the problem, he advised that the woman should consult a lawyer.

They discussed it some more. The real estate person told her that *probably* she did not owe any money, but reiterated that she would need an attorney to extricate herself from this troublesome situation.

My analysis of this case is different from that of the guest on the radio talk show. A legitimate lien is *always* accompanied by papers. There were no papers evidencing the lien. There was never a contract. The contact of the woman's daughter by the "contractor" would have made me smell a rat in an instant. This case has none of the trappings of the actions of a professional contractor, and it has all the earmarks of the actions of a confidence man.

When he spoke to her, he had pumped her for information. That is how he learned how to reach her daughter.

The caller had no reason to spend her money on an attorney. She should have been advised to contact the police or the consumer fraud department of her city or county.

The good news is that any reputable attorney, on hearing this case, would instantly smell a fraud, and would undoubtedly point the woman in the direction of the law enforcement authorities. Thus, her total loss from the real estate agent's advice would have been the initial fee to the lawyer, plus, of course, the additional grief she would have suffered in the meantime.

There was no need for her to have the anxiety of anticipating a contested legal action, requiring that each side present its case. Clearly the "contractor" was no contractor. He was a despicable fraud. And the fact that he was a fraud was, at least to me, blindingly obvious from the facts of the case, as recounted by the woman. She would not have had to pay one penny to anyone on this matter.

Most of us are accustomed to dealing with people in an honorable manner. Not being either trained in or accustomed to swindling deception, the idea that someone we have met is an out-an-out lying, thieving crook may never occur to us. The very knowledgeable real estate expert apparently saw this as a messy contractual dispute. The clear (to me) fact that it was a deliberate, calculated fraud evidently never even entered his mind . . . or if it did, he did not know how to deal with it.

Chapter 16

And the Beat Goes On

You don't get a tax deduction for the use of a prostitute.
Larry Wright, Internal Revenue Service (news interview, San Francisco, May 9, 1989).

The above announcement addresses a topic that would seem to be too foolish to have any serious import. While we can agree that the topic *should be* too foolish to even contemplate, allow me to assure you that the foolishness was not on the part of Mr. Wright. The foolishness was on the part of "astute business people" who actually took such a deduction.

The prostitution ring, which was busted, operated under make-believe business names which sounded like legitimate businesses. They took credit cards. The business people deducted the charges as computer software, or as other legitimate-sounding business expenses.

We are not here to discuss the tax system itself. However, this *is* the proper forum for me to advise you how not to get burned.

It is generally a good idea on your income tax returns to take all the deductions to which you are legitimately entitled. If you have an honest disagreement with Internal Revenue Service over interpretation of the law, it is sometimes a good idea, on the advice of your tax advisor, to take the deductions anyway, and to prepare to do battle. Sometimes it is even wise to take your case to the courts. I am a practicing certified public accountant. That advice comes from decades of thinking about and doing those very things on behalf of clients.

Tax evasion is, as the expression goes, "a whole nother matter." Deducting the cost of a prostitute, failing to report taxable income, failing to file income tax returns, fraudulently inflating deductions, and many other such tactics come under the heading of tax evasion.

You will not run short of people advising you to evade taxes: they hold seminars and they write books. The advice they give is glib and seductive. Irwin Schiff is the author of many books on tax resistance. He is bright and an eloquent speaker. His presentations and his book *How Anyone Can Stop Paying Income Taxes* (Schiff and Murzin 1982) are enticing. When he assures you that "no American is legally required to file an income tax return" (Schiff and Murzin 1982, 12), you want to believe it.

In considering whether to follow his advice, would it change your thinking at all to know that he has served time in federal prison for tax evasion? Many of the purveyors of the "easy way" to never pay taxes have served time in prison.

Some advise that you do not file tax returns at all, and that you simply keep a low profile. "They will never find you," you are assured. Well, how about that? Are there people out there who do not file, do not get audited, and do not go to prison? Yes, there are. But they pay a very heavy price! They live their lives in the shadows. They do not legally, on the record, own anything. They do their business "off the books." They live their lives as if they were being hunted at all times.

Furthermore, some people refuse to deal with them, on principle. Other people are afraid to deal with them in business, for fear of being caught in tax evasion. Those who do deal with them accept that they cannot take deductions for the amounts paid. Therefore, lacking the ability to take the deduction, they negotiate a lower price. The seller, the tax evader, thus earns far less than he or she otherwise could.

Tax evasion is a way of life, and a very unhappy one. All your life, every day, you live with the knowledge that the sword may drop on your head at any moment, bringing you to financial ruin, sending you to prison, and bringing shame to you and those you love.

I have seen the grief it has brought to many. In addition to the price of grief, often they end up paying a greater price in money than if they had properly filed all along.

It is the United States Congress and the President that make all of the Federal Income Tax laws. Those are the people with whom we must do battle if we actually expect to change the injustices in our tax system. To complain about an unjust tax law to an Internal Revenue Service agent is like arguing with a policeman about an unjust speed limit. Take your battle about the laws to those who pass the laws. We have a representative form of government, with elections. If we do not like what our representatives do, we can and should vote them out.

Meanwhile, to evade taxes because you do not like the rules does not make sense.

I am not moralizing. I am merely expressing my opinion that tax evasion is a stupid, costly, destructive way to live your life.

✳ ✳ ✳ ✳ ✳ ✳

Speaking of Internal Revenue Service, suppose an IRS agent knocks on your door. He informs you that you have been selected for audit. You panic. He is willing to negotiate a settlement. If you will make out a check for $700.00 to IRS, he will give you a signed release and close the audit. You will get an audit report disclosing the settlement within a week. You view that as a bargain, so you give him the check. After all, with a check made out to IRS, it has to be for real.

Guess what? You have been taken. That "IRS agent" was not an IRS agent. He was a con artist, posing as an agent of the Internal Revenue Service.

Surprise visits by Internal Revenue Service to a long-time tax evader are a possibility. Surprise visits as the first contact are unheard of. Don't get taken!

✳ ✳ ✳ ✳ ✳ ✳

When you pay your tax bill to the United States Government, you should make the check out to "IRS," right? Wrong! Every year many such checks are stolen from the mails, plus many con artist posing as Internal Revenue Service Agents obtain checks made out to IRS. The checks are then fraudulently endorsed with names such as "I. R. Smith," and cashed. Internal Revenue Service does not receive the payment, so your account stands as it did before you wrote that check. Take the few extra seconds to make your check out to "Internal Revenue Service." The same holds true for other checks, such as to the telephone or utility company.

❋ ❋ ❋ ❋ ❋ ❋

You may meet "her" at the Hotel Splendide, on the beaches at Deauville, or in the sporting club at Monte Carlo, and she may tell you, if you are a man of the world (or even if you are not) that you are a very remarkable person. And you will believe it. She will then tell you that you are very wise. And you will, of course, believe that. And then, one day, when you look into your pocketbook, you will say to yourself, "I was not so wise" (Lucas 1927, v-vi).

If you have been on this planet for a while, you have most assuredly run into people whom you considered to be friends and lovers who turned out to be manipulators. Now don't go sexist on me: neither men nor women have a monopoly on this devious skill.

Some people fine-tune the talent, and set about taking on the world. Others simply fine-tune the talent to trap just one person.

It is devastating to learn that the person whom you trusted and deeply loved was after you only for your money, prestige, looks, and/or to enable the person to become a mother, a father, and/or a citizen. It was all an act. Sometimes the act continues undetected for months, years, or even for a lifetime.

❋ ❋ ❋ ❋ ❋ ❋

"Good afternoon, Mrs. Jones. This is Mike Daniels, at the Post Office. We have a package for you. Will you be able to come down some time today to pick it up?"

Do not go! The United States Postal Service rarely, if ever, makes such a call. If you go, you are in for three surprises. When you arrive at the Post Office you will find that 1) they did not make the call, and 2) there is no employee named Mike Daniels working there. 3) The third surprise comes when you return home to find that your home has been burglarized in your absence.

＊ ＊ ＊ ＊ ＊ ＊

You are home alone when the doorbell rings. When you answer it, the three people represent themselves to be, and appear to be, a grandmother, a mother, and a little baby crying in her mother's arms.

"We're terribly sorry to trouble you, but my grand-daughter is very thirsty. Could we please just fill her bottle with cold water?"

How can you refuse? So you invite them in. The mother and baby go into the kitchen with you, while you chat and tend to the chore of filling the baby's bottle. Then you admire the baby, and comment on how cute she is, as you watch her guzzle the water. Her crying has stopped, and you are pleased.

They thank you profusely, and leave.

That's all there is to it. What's that? You left your wallet on the coffee table in the living room, and now it is gone? And your gold watch, too?

While you, mother, and baby were in the kitchen, "grandma" was loading up her purse with your wallet, gold watch, antiques, silver, and that diamond brooch you bought to surprise your granddaughter on her graduation from medical school.

Now all you folks who admire the "noble" con artists, who say that victims deserve what they get, and who say that people can only be taken because they are basically greedy or dishonest, what say you now?

＊ ＊ ＊ ＊ ＊ ＊

"Hey buddy, this gold watch is worth $800.00. I have to catch an airplane to Phoenix and have to buy the ticket. I'll let you have the watch for only $200.00."

You question if the watch is stolen. He replies, "Shhhh! Let's not discuss that. I gotta go. Do you want it or not? It's cheap."

If you buy it, you will find that the "cheap stolen gold" watch is none of those things: The price was not cheap, the watch was not stolen, and it is not gold. The jeweler tells you it is worth about $17.00.

Don't be a sucker.

❋ ❋ ❋ ❋ ❋ ❋

The brochure has some beautiful pictures of prime land. "Buy this wonderful land in Florida. You will pay only $83.19 per month, for the next 10 years. At the end of that time, you will own the land. The interest rate is only 4%: far less that you pay on most mortgages."

Many people who sign up on this type of deal never visit the property and never carefully read the contract. Some of this land is undeveloped: there are no sewers, telephone, gas, or electricity available, and it may even be swampland. Furthermore, if you default just once in the 120 months of the contract, you lose everything.

They claim as a selling point that the interest rate is lower than on other mortgages. There is, however, a fundamental difference. When you buy a house and contract to pay a mortgage on it, you are living in the house. You have the use of the property.

If you were to put money into a savings account each month, saving toward a future purchase, the savings institution would pay you interest on your account. In the "marvelous land deal," you are putting money away for a future purchase, and you are paying them interest. You are paying for the privilege of saving your own money for a future investment. And if you miss one payment into your savings plan, they take all of your money.

It is a terrible deal. Stay away.

❋ ❋ ❋ ❋ ❋ ❋

Many advertisements for devices, creams, and pills imply that they will aid your sexual appearance and perfor-

mance. They show pictures of well-endowed men and
women. However, beyond the innuendoes and the seductive
pictures, a careful reading of the words will tell you that
they are in fact not making any claim whatsoever. Let us
examine a few of the ads.

> Can VACUUM PUMPS permanently ENLARGE your
> PENIS? Doctors say "NO!" The F.D.A. says "NO!" In
> spite of the statements made by government and physi-
> cians, OVER 1 MILLION VACUUM PUMPS are sold
> EVERY YEAR!

Read what that says. Physicians and the United States
Food and Drug Administration say "NO!" The purveyor
does not counter the "NO!" statements, but merely tells you
that they are selling the item. They go on to state:

> We have received countless letters over the years from
> satisfied users with some claiming incredible results.
> However, we are not allowed, by law, to make any
> claims whatsoever as to the results you may obtain
> from the use of these devices.

If you read an ad for aspirin, it will clearly make claims
about what it will do. The pump folks are not allowed, by
law, to make any claims for one reason, and for one reason
only: their product has never demonstrated any effective
results. Any manufacturer whose product has been tested
and found to be safe and effective can most assuredly
lawfully make claims as to expected results. The only
restriction (Got that?—the *ONLY* restriction) is that the
claims must be true. If the pump people had a valid, true,
scientific claim, you had better believe that they would tell
you all about it.

The ad for "Spanish Fly Drops" and "Nymphomaniac
Drops" states:

> The MOST POWERFUL inert liquid formulations on
> the market. We keep selling them because the demand
> is so great!

"Inert" means inactive. It has no effect whatsoever. Their statement that they keep selling them because the demand is so great is quite accurate. But the drops do not *do* anything from the medical or scientific point of view.

There are many more examples that could be given. If I were to detail some of them, this book would become X-rated.

I have inquired of both attorneys and physicians about why these items are allowed on the market. The answer is that the sellers do not misrepresent; they make no false claims. The way they make no false claims is by not making any claims whatsoever as to the effectiveness of the products.

Here, as in many of the other items covered, no specialized knowledge is required on your part. A careful reading of the ads will show you that no claim of effectiveness is shown. If there are any words that are unfamiliar to you, look them up in the dictionary. Advertisers of ineffective products will frequently use unfamiliar words, hoping that you will not understand them. For example, I have here an ad for "Postiche Spanish Fly Sugar." *Postiche* means "artificial, false." I have seen ads for "faux diamonds." *Faux* is a French word; its English translation is "false, bogus, fake."

❋ ❋ ❋ ❋ ❋ ❋

Mail fraud finds its way into homes and businesses throughout the world. The pyramid scheme we have seen is just one of them. Another is the work-at-home scam, where the promoters promise you a great deal of money with "no investment necessary," and with little work on your part.

Take a Bite Out of Crime—A Consumer's Guide to Postal Crime Prevention deals with this, as well as many other forms of postal fraud. I highly recommend that you get a copy of this booklet. It is free, from the United States

Postal Service, Postal Inspection Service, Washington, DC 20260-2186. Please tell them I sent you.

About the work-at-home scams, that booklet states:

> *Beware:* Work-at-home schemes will not guarantee regular salaried employment. They *will* require you to invest your money before explaining how a plan works or before you are sent instructions. The work you are asked to do often continues the fraud by getting other victims involved. Always suspect any ad claiming you can earn unusually high income with little or no effort on your part (United States Postal Inspection Service 1979, 7).

The "no investment necessary" claim in the ads is, in a word, fraudulent.

❉ ❉ ❉ ❉ ❉ ❉

You were recently widowed; your spouse died just two days ago. The doorbell rings. There is a package for you from your late spouse. It is gift-wrapped. The delivery person informs you that it has been sent C.O.D.: you owe $35.70.

It appears to be one of the last acts of your beloved, departed spouse. You pay the $35.70 in cash. When you open the package, you discover only crumpled newspapers. The con artist had read the obituary notice in the paper and conned you. He took advantage of your grief.

❉ ❉ ❉ ❉ ❉ ❉

There are investment frauds out there that have taken in and defrauded some of the finest minds in the country. Real estate, securities, stocks, bonds, gold, and insurance scams are just some of them. What looks like a golden opportunity turns out to be phony. Take the time to investigate any business, investment, or job opportunities that come along. Do not be hasty.

❉ ❉ ❉ ❉ ❉ ❉

When you get a solicitation from a charity—by mail, telephone, or in person—be sure to check to determine if it is a legitimate charity. There are a lot of cons out there posing as workers for charity.

❊ ❊ ❊ ❊ ❊ ❊

There are more, many more cons that may greet you in life. Now you have the basics about what to question and what to think about.

Let us move on to point out some of the most dreadful cons in the world. Then we will close with a section (more of a review and summing up) on how to protect yourself and those you love against bunco and bunkum. Stay tuned.

PART IV

THE CRUELEST CONS

Chapter 17

Psychic Surgery

True hope dwells on the possible. . . . True hope responds to the real world, real life; it is an active effort. False hope, on the other hand, is dangerous; it's pathological.
Courage Is a Three-Letter Word (Anderson 1986, 33).

Psychic surgery is claimed as a medical miracle. It is performed in the Philippines, as well as elsewhere around the world. It is illegal in the United States, but is performed nonetheless. Recently in California, a practitioner was convicted and sentenced to prison.

The psychic surgeon "operates" on a patient, apparently removing the offending part (for example, cancer) from the patient's body. Frequently this is done without making an incision. It is, so we are instructed to believe, done miraculously, psychically.

In case the above seems a bit unclear, allow me to present an explanation presented by a believer. Tom Valen-

117

tine, in his book entitled *Psychic Surgery*, offers the following:

> A spirit entity has the same free will possessed by an
> incarnate entity. . . . A spirit trained in medicine while
> incarnate and able to perceive the vital body function
> as a decarnate can perform successful psychic surgery.
>
> In order to establish the mediumistic rapport the entity
> needs a willing subject (Valentine 1973, 153-154).

After continuing with more of the same, Valentine concludes:

> These mechanics of mediumship have been presented
> in an oversimplified form, but essentially this is how
> psychic surgery works (Valentine 1973, 155).

Let us put this into perspective. I have studied, investigated, understand, have performed, and will continue to perform psychic surgery. In my presentations, I do not pretend that it is real. I do it as an exposé at hospitals, medical conferences, scientific conferences, law enforcement seminars, and for citizens' groups. Richard P. Wheat, M.D., in an open letter, states:

> Mr. Steiner, as part of a program . . . on Cancer Fraud,
> gave a fascinating presentation of psychic surgery—
> how it works, and how easily people can be bewitched
> by this form of magic. He was able to fool our audience
> of physicians and to explain the mechanisms which are
> utilized in this cancer quackery. His presentation is
> excellent and he was very well received by our staff. I
> am happy to recommend this presentation.

From the top: Psychic surgery is a fraud. It is, quite simply, a magic trick.

For centuries audiences have viewed the entertainment art form known as magic and have reveled in the joy of the illusions.

These same skills, misused, are an integral part of one of the cruelest cons on the face of the earth.

Suppose you were to see a performing magician apparently turn a beautiful woman into a full-grown Bengal tiger. Do you know how it is done? Unless you have studied the art of magic or are unusually perceptive, probably not. How about pulling a rabbit out of a hat? Same answer.

And yet, you do not consider these effects to be miracles (at least I hope you do not). During the performance, you may allow yourself to suspend your disbelief. You will permit yourself to be a child and to enjoy the surprises and joys of being fooled and entertained.

However, at the most fundamental level, you are aware that everything is done by normal means. There are no supernatural forces at work.

On the other hand, some observers see a psychic surgeon apparently pull a diseased tumor out of a patient without having made an incision, and are willing to swear that they have witnessed a miracle.

For the record, my ability to fool the physicians quoted above refers to the fact that, although they watched closely, they did not detect *how* I performed the trickery. They knew all along that it *was* trickery.

The psychic surgeons prey primarily on those who believe that there is no remaining help to be received from the "medical establishment." Medical mystics put a great deal of effort into making it an us-them adversarial position. They claim that the "medical establishment" is getting wealthy, while squelching information about alternative medical treatments and "miracle cures."

When someone has been diagnosed as having terminal cancer (for example), that person is very ripe to be taken by the medical grifters. The patient figures, "What have I got to lose?"

To answer that, suppose we pose the question a different way. If you probably were terminally ill, which would you prefer: A) to frenetically run about, throwing away your time and money, using up your remaining energy, all in the pursuit of a false hope, or B) to give the true medical professionals their best shot at improving your health, while you spend time with friends and loved ones, or maybe even getting your affairs in order? Or, still under category "B," you could choose to spend your time, money, and energy doing things you always wanted to do: take that trip to the islands, write a book, or follow any of a host of other pursuits.

The reports you hear of psychic surgery from friends and often in the media are glowing endorsements. Yet the scientific support for and validation of the procedure are totally lacking. This bears a little investigation. Let us look at the various types of people who go for this claimed miraculous treatment.

Some persons who go have not been properly diagnosed by responsible medical professionals. Medical mystics have been known to "diagnose" diseases which do not exist in the patients. Then, after doing their mumbo jumbo, the psychic surgeons will pronounce the patients cured. But they have "cured" a "disease" that did not exist. The patients are elated and return home to give sparkling testimonials.

Sometimes a patient receives a treatment which has no proven therapeutic effect, but the person's belief in the treatment will cause positive medical results. This includes cases where diseases are psychosomatic or psychological. It can take place in a person who undergoes the make-believe medical treatment called psychic surgery. These people happily give testimonials.

This positive medical help as a result of the patient's belief is called the *placebo effect*. According to laboratory tests, there is real medical improvement. Depending upon the disease, the placebo effect can take place in as much as 30% of the cases.

Some argue that that alone is enough reason to justify psychic surgery. However, there is a problem with that thinking.

If you go to a professional physician, he or she may diagnose that you have a fairly common disease. There may be a medicine that will solve the problem. A prescription is given, and you will be cured. There are many medical and surgical procedures that will cure, improve, or alleviate medical problems. As a last resort, if all else fails, the medical professional can still try a placebo. In other words, a placebo is *one* of the weapons in the professional's arsenal to fight disease.

The mystic, on the other hand, has *only* placebo. If you have a standard disease that can be cured by a standard medicine, you are out of luck if you visit the mystic.

Hypochondriacs get their kicks and attention in life by monopolizing conversations with complaints of minor or non-existent ailments. When such a person returns home after psychic surgery, he or she can attract and hold a large, enthusiastic audience in the social milieu by recounting the glowing tales of the "miraculous cure" under the magic hands of the psychic surgeon.

A small percentage of the "cures" are the result of spontaneous remissions. These occur with or without the psychic surgery. In order to attribute any causation or benefit to the mystical treatment, we would have to establish that such remissions take place in a higher proportion of the patients who go for psychic surgery than in those who do not. No such statistics have been presented. Thus, the scientific conclusion is that the mystical treatment has not been validated. However, the personal, subjective conclusion of the person who traveled to the Philippines for the miracle cure is that the miracle of psychic surgery has indeed taken place. These people willingly give testimonials.

Another group consists of those who make the trip and pay the money for psychic surgery, and show no improvement. They are frequently too embarrassed and too ashamed to admit that they were taken. So they say nothing.

Many terminally ill people go to the Philippines for psychic surgery, return home in a euphoric mood, believing that they were cured, and then very shortly die.

Now you know why you hear mostly lofty testimonials endorsing the miracles of psychic surgery. Those who realize they have been taken rarely complain. The dead never complain.

Unlike many other mystical claims and beliefs discussed in this book, there is no room for questioning the sincerity of the perpetrators of psychic surgery. Before the show (They call it "surgery," but it is in fact a theatrical performance.), they physically hide the material which they will later seem to remove from the patient. Then, by sleight-of-hand, misdirection, or by any of the other wonderful-when-properly-used-for-entertainment-purposes skills of a magician, they physically produce the materials. Sorry folks: with such carefully planned and calculated deception, there is no room to plead that they are innocent and sincere. They are lying, thieving, cheating, unscrupulous con artists perpetrating grotesque fraud on those who are innocent and desperately ill.

Chapter 18

The Faith Healers

My grandfather was a minister. When my grandmother was diagnosed as being a diabetic, they turned to faith healers. They attended all sorts of revivals, hoping to cure her illness. Thinking she had been cured, she consumed [foods her doctors had advised against], which eventually killed her. She died on my birthday.

Name withheld by request.

The claims made by faith-healers are nothing more than hollow boasts and do not stand up to examination. Prepared culturally to expect miracles, convinced they are helpless without supernatural intervention, and bullied into supporting their gurus far beyond their means, the pathetic victims of the healers have become a disillusioned subculture playing a dangerous game. "The Healing Show," with its cruel lies, vain promises, and glittering trickery, has blinded them to reality and removed them from productive society. They are the dupes of clever, glib, highly organized swindlers who are immune from justice and are confidently aware of that fact.

The Faith Healers (Randi 1987, 292).

A ten-year-old boy on crutches came to the Peter Popoff Crusade in San Francisco. Although his legs were twisted, his head was held high and his spirit was buoyant. He expressed confidence that he would be healed that day. Upon probing, we learn that he believed that the healing would be done by Jesus Christ, working through Reverend Peter Popoff. In reply to a question as to why he believed that, the boy expressed unquestioning faith in asserting that it was because Reverend Popoff understands Jesus.

The next time we saw the lad was after the crusade. He was still on crutches, his legs were still twisted, but he no longer exhibited the enthusiasm he had shown just hours earlier. Now his shoulders were slumped, his head was bowed, his eyes were looking down, and tears were streaming down his cheeks.

His spirit was broken. He had just joined the ranks of the hundreds of thousands, perhaps millions, of people who have been taken in by the cruel, empty promises of the faith healers.

Hundreds of millions of dollars go to the faith healers each year. In return for that, they put on a show in which they apparently heal people of diseases.

James Randi did a major investigation of the faith healers. For the definitive report on the subject, I heartily recommend for your information *The Faith Healers*, by James Randi (Randi 1987). I was pleased to be an active participant in that investigation.

Peter Popoff, in his crusade, would call out names of people in the audience. He would tell them of their diseases, name their doctors, give their addresses, and more. He specifically and clearly claimed that the information was given to him directly by God.

In fact, the information was given to him by his wife Elizabeth Popoff. She was backstage, broadcasting the information. It was received by Peter Popoff in the small receiver he had deep within his ear.

How do I know this? you may ask. Because I was with Alec Jason, electronics expert, when he tapped into the broadcasts from Elizabeth Popoff to Peter Popoff. The following excerpt was taken, with permission, from my article "Exposing the Faith-Healers," published in *The Skeptical Inquirer* (Steiner 1986, 29-30):

> The information for Popoff's so-called healings among the audience came from secret radio transmissions from Elizabeth Popoff backstage. She obtained the information from "prayer cards" filled out by the attendees, as well as from her conversations with those present before the start of the formal proceedings. The Reverend Popoff then reveals the information to the assembled crowd as divine messages from God.
>
> The following example of a healing was taken from our tape of the Popoff Crusade . . . in Anaheim, California, on March 16, 1986.
>
> Peter Popoff calls out: "Virgil. Is it Jorgenson? Who is Virgil?"
>
> After a man in the audience identified himself as Jorgenson, Popoff continued: "Are you ready for God to overhaul those knees?"
>
> The spectator appeared to be in his sixties and walked with a cane. When he reacted to Popoff's "healing," Popoff went on: "Oh, glory to God. I'll tell you, God's going to touch that sister of yours all the way over in Sweden."
>
> Popoff then took the . . . cane and broke it over his . . . knee. The spectator walked about the auditorium, praising Popoff and God.

Now let's look behind the scenes. With the benefit of our electronics technology, we hear the entire conversation.

Elizabeth Popoff transmits to Peter Popoff: "Virgil Jorgenson. Virgil."

Peter Popoff calls out "Virgil."

Elizabeth: "Jorgenson."

Peter (inquiringly): "Is it Jorgenson?"

Elizabeth: "Way back in the back somewhere. Arthritis in knees. He's got a cane."

Peter: "Who is Virgil?"

Elizabeth: "He's got a cane."

Peter: Are you ready for God to overhaul those knees?"

Elizabeth: "He's got arthritis. He's praying for his sister in Sweden, too."

Peter: "Oh, glory to God. I'll tell you, God's going to touch that sister of yours all the way over in Sweden."

There are many more such conversations on our tapes.

So impressive was the "healing" of Virgil Jorgenson that Peter Popoff used the film clip for three consecutive weeks on his television show.

Popoff assures the folks forcefully and often that his information comes directly from God. As a matter of fact, he even claims to have visited Heaven for some weeks and to have personally spoken to God.

An important part of our investigation . . . was to obtain proof not only that Popoff's claimed method of obtaining information was false, but also that the information itself is sometimes false. This would strengthen our case in proving that the information does not, as claimed, come from God. Enter Don Henvick.

While we could devote an entire book to the strange and exciting escapades of Don Henvick, we will give just a few highlights.

Working with us, Don went to the Popoff Crusade in San Francisco. Don was about 40 years of age, with a full head of hair, a beard, and a mustache. Popoff selected him as one of about 15 people to "heal," from an audience of about 1,800 people. Don used the name Tom Hendrys, and was "healed" of the problem of alcoholism. Don is not an alcoholic and does not have a drinking problem.

A few days later, several of us traveled to Stockton, California, for the crusade of Reverend David Paul. Of about 800 people, 10 were selected for "healing." Don was among them, again as Tom Hendrys, alcoholic.

The following month we traveled to Anaheim, California, for another Popoff crusade. We assumed that Don would not be healed again, since he might be recognized. Oh, how we underestimated the creativity and acting ability of Don Henvick. He shaved his head, and shaved off his beard and mustache. With white powder on the bit of hair remaining on his head, and adorned with a cane, Don became a new person—Virgil Jorgenson, to be exact. As Virgil, he was "healed" of crippling arthritis. So good was this healing that Popoff put it on his television show three weeks in a row. By the way, Don is a mail carrier. He walks many miles several days a week. He does not have arthritis.

Soon thereafter we went to Philadelphia for the crusade of Reverend W. V. Grant. Of approximately 2,500 people, 32 were selected for healing. Yup, Don was among them. That day he was Abel McMinn, and was "healed" of a prostate condition and arthritis, neither of which he has.

Now came the challenge. Don was going to Detroit, for a Peter Popoff Crusade. He had been healed by Popoff twice, and had appeared on Popoff's television show thrice. Would Don be equal to this challenge? What do you think?

In Detroit, Popoff "healed" a woman named Bernice Manicoff of uterine cancer. After the "healing," Popoff had Ms. Manicoff get up out of her wheelchair and walk. "Bernice Manicoff" was Don Henvick! Need I point out that Don does not have uterine cancer?

The odds seemed to be stacked against me. I had agreed to appear on a television show in San Francisco with faith healer Grace DiBiccari, who calls herself "Amazing Grace." The agreed-upon format was that, on segment one, Grace would be interviewed. Segment two would consist of her doing "healings." I was to be introduced in segment three, where I would share the platform with Grace.

Friends advised me to cancel my appearance. Since all the advance promotion had been about Amazing Grace, the audience would consist of her followers and true believers. She would be interviewed. Then she would do her demonstration. Friends theorized that, by that time, I would be lost. Everybody would hate me, and I would not have a chance of getting across any point at all.

I honored the appearance. Furthermore, I was able to get my point across, in spades. I was able, with confidence, to point out that Grace had committed the ultimate blasphemy, and that she was a false prophet. How did I manage all of that? I brought along my secret weapon. What was my secret weapon? Why, Don Henvick, of course. Don was the first person Grace "healed," "healing" him of a non-existent disease.

The point in spending time telling about the "healings" of Don Henvick is for you to consider that in light of the fact that all of the faith healers claim that their information comes from God. When asked, all of them assure us that God never makes an error.

Thus, when they profess to heal a person of a disease, and when they have the wrong name of that person, and when the person does not have the disease mentioned, we have proven beyond a reasonable doubt that the faith healer is a liar, a fraud, a swindler, a false prophet, and is blaspheming the name and the entire concept of God.

The danger of the faith healers is incalculable. In addition to taking money from the sick and the desperate, they keep those people away from real health professionals who might well be able to help them.

But it does not end there. They give specific instructions which could kill members of the audience, and the audience-members follow the advice:

> Popoff . . . spoke to his audience about the terrible doctors who were asking them to put "chemicals" in their bodies. "Dr. Jesus doesn't *use* any chemicals!" he screamed. And he told them to come forward and throw their medications up on the stage. They did. When I examined those substances, I found—among other medications—nitroglycerin tablets, insulin, and digitalis compounds. These are substances without which those people might well die (Randi 1987, 298).

One would think that such con artists would be prosecuted and sent to prison. Not so. The law enforcement people will not touch them. As to why, I cannot answer. I agree with James Randi when he calls it "a dangerous and insidious legal situation that needs attention from the Supreme Court of this land" (Randi 1987, 298).

As for you, the best advice I can give you is to stay away from the faith healers. They are dangerous, unscrupulous people. They will take your money, your time, your health, and maybe even your life. We will close with the words of James Randi, from his excellent book *The Faith Healers* (Randi 1987, 268):

By teaching people dependence on magical practices, faith-healers take them back to the Dark Ages, convincing them that they are only pawns in some great game they cannot comprehend. . . . Faith-healers take from their subjects any hope of managing on their own. And they may well take them away from legitimate treatments that could really help them.

Chapter 19

Other "Medical Miracles"

A man in Montana who called himself a nature healer convinced the parents of a 16-year-old diabetic girl that her daily insulin shots were unnecessary. By tapping the chest, he said, he could stimulate their daughter's own insulin-making capacity. Three days later, the girl was dead. Her parents were billed $6,350 for the treatment.

"Beware the Health Hucksters" (Michelmore 1989, 114).

Quackery is the promotion of questionable health products and services (questionableness pertaining to safety and/or effectiveness). People who fit such a description are quacks whether they are sincere or fraudulent, medical doctors or impostors, operating within the law or not.

Quackery and You (Jarvis 1983, 7).

t is important to understand and recognize the broad spectrum of people who are quacks. Professor Jarvis, President of the National Council Against Health Fraud, in his booklet *Quackery and You* (quoted above), gives the parameters. Please note that quacks may be fraudulent (practicing bunco) or sincere (selling bunkum). The National Council Against Health Fraud (listed in Resources) is an excellent source of information on medical quackery.

It is no simple matter to spot quacks. We must constantly remain aware and alert. Quacks may be licensed as professionals and may be operating within the law. Or, of course, they may be illegally practicing medicine without a license.

James A. Lowell, Ph.D., a knowledgeable medical researcher, points out an interesting theme seen throughout the world of quackery:

> Unorthodox healers often claim to be persecuted. It seems that whenever an alternative or unorthodox healing method is questioned by any branch of the "establishment," the cry of "foul" is heard. The practitioner or promoter claims that he is a scientist ahead of his time, and that the establishment is trying to suppress his great medical discovery in order to protect its own economic monopoly on health care (Lowell 1987, 66).

John A. Richardson, M.D., and Patricia Griffin, R.N., in *Laetrile Case Histories*, give a fine example of Dr. Lowell's statement:

> The "proven cures" of the American Cancer Society do not exist. In view of the record, they are an affront to our intelligence, and they constitute one of the most tragic myths of the Twentieth Century. Undoubtedly they are useful for fund-raising purposes but they cannot be supported by the scientific record.
>
> This myth is one of the assumptions used to justify government action against those who wish to use Laetrile. It is one of the assumptions that has caused respected physicians—whose only crime is that perhaps they are ahead of their time—to be subjected to legal harassment, ruinous publicity, professional sanctions, fines, and actual punishment (Richardson & Griffin 1977, 65).

Victor Herbert, M.D., J.D., and Stephen Barrett, M.D., are in the forefront of investigation of medical quackery. Having studied the subject, they sum up laetrile as follows: "Laetrile heads the all-time list of quack cancer remedies" (Herbert and Barrett 1981, 108).

A recital of the investigations, trials, convictions, and censures of the proponents and purveyors of laetrile would fill this book. Some physicians have been threatened with suspension of medical licenses, loss of hospital privileges, and legal prosecution. Others have in fact stood trial. Convictions have resulted in fines, prison time, probation, and suspension of medical licenses. Non-physicians have been convicted of practicing medicine without a license.

Laetrile has been promoted as a way to prevent cancer, to manage cancer, and to cure cancer. It has been labeled "Vitamin B-17" by its promoters. It is *not* a vitamin!

The track record of laetrile in the prevention and treatment of cancer is clear: it has been scientifically tested. It has failed to prove that it is safe—people have died from its use. It has failed to prove that it is effective—there is no clinical evidence that it can help to prevent cancer, manage cancer, or cure cancer. It does not relieve the pain or other symptoms of cancer. It is dangerous. It can kill you! Laetrile contains cyanide; it is poison. I repeat—it can kill you. "Researchers have recorded dozens of deaths and poisonings from the cyanide in vitamin B-17" (Lowell 1987, 109).

The greatest danger from the use of laetrile is that it keeps the patient away from reputable health professionals who might be able to help.

> Unfortunately, many patients with curable cancer leave the care of competent physicians to be treated with a worthless unproven remedy until a cure by accepted methods of treatment becomes impossible. . . . Time is cancer's ally. Any time wasted on worthless unproven remedies may prevent a patient from obtaining proven treatment while his cancer is still curable (Richardson

and Griffin 1977, 44. It is interesting that these laetrile promoters quote the above from publications by the American Cancer Society.).

An especially tragic case of poisoning occurred in 1978 when a 17-year-old California girl drank an ounce of laetrile. A malignant tumor on her lung had been removed by surgery, but "to be safe" she went to Mexico and bought the poison that is illegal in California. Within ten minutes she became dizzy and developed a headache. She went into convulsions, lapsed into a coma, and was dead within a day. Ironically, an autopsy showed that not only had she died of cyanide poisoning but that her diagnosed cancer had been cured by the surgery (Lowell 1987, 109).

Many other medical "miracles" also claim quick, easy, painless cures.

Whenever there is a claimed cure for a disease from which many people continue to suffer, be on guard. Let us look at two examples.

Example One. You do not hear wild claims about exotic methods to prevent polio, accompanied by the claim that "the medical establishment" is hiding the miracle in order to make money. Why not? Because there is a real, scientifically tested method to prevent polio. It works! Physicians ("the medical establishment," if you must), rather than attempting to cover it up, wholeheartedly endorse the outcome of the research. They are delighted with the results.

That should come as no surprise to anyone who takes the trouble to actually think about it. After all, physicians are human beings. They have feelings, thoughts, responsibilities, and fears—just like the rest of us. They do not want their children to contract polio, any more than you would want your children to contract this dreaded disease.

Example Two. Arthritis is a disease for which, at the present time, there is no known method of prevention or cure. Result: Enter the quacks. The tabloids are loaded with ads for "miracle" cures for arthritis which, it is claimed, "the medical establishment" does not use, tries to stop, or does not know about.

Think about that. Physicians and their families get diseases. They may suffer from arthritis, just like the rest of us. Why on earth would they cover up a known prevention or cure to this crippling disease? Answer: They would not. It is absurd to think that they would.

Conclusion: Beware of "secret" or "mystical" or "alternative" treatments and cures which "the medical establishment" does not use. It does not make a whole lot of sense that such things exist.

We have explored in some depth one example of a claimed medical miracle—laetrile. It has been falsely touted as a prevention, relief, and cure of cancer. We have seen the absurdity of the notion that physicians would try to hide safe and effective cures known to them.

The massive doses of vitamins promoted by the health hustlers will definitely cost you money, might harm you, and, unless you have a specific need for extra vitamins, will probably not do you any good.

It is easy to understand why someone who has contracted AIDS would desperately try anything. There are many touted "cures" for AIDS. The medical research, as of this writing, has not found a cure.

Iridology is a claimed method of diagnosing a patient's medical problems by looking at the iris of the eye. In scientific tests, it has failed to prove accuracy beyond what one would expect by chance. It is bunkum.

Reflexology proponents claim that there are "meridians" going throughout the body which culminate in the hands and the feet. For example, reflexologists claim (and apparently most of them sincerely believe) that massaging the outside of the big toe—either big toe—will solve problems in your nose. If you rub the bone on the outside of the left

ankle, you can alleviate problems in the vagina or penis—
presumably you would have to briefly investigate the rest
of the patient to determine which.

Many useless medical devices flood the market, ranging
from a claimed breakthrough system to attack the common
cold to cures for more serious diseases.

There are many, many more areas of claimed miraculous medical cures.

For each claimed miracle, ask yourself the question: If
it is so good, how come professional physicians do not
endorse it? Remember, they and their families can get sick,
too.

Before leaving this chapter, I would like to give one
more reinforcement that bunkum can do you in as easily as
bunco. I again stress that someone who is sincere *and wrong*
can harm you just as much as the dedicated, fraudulent
criminal.

> Many people who promote unproven methods of can-
> cer management are well-meaning individuals who are
> sincere in their beliefs. The rest are profiteers. Regard-
> less of their motivation, however, one thing is clear.
> Incurable cancer patients who waste their life's savings
> on false hopes, and potentially curable patients who die
> from delay of proper treatment, are victims of quackery
> at its cruelest (Wood and Presley 1980, 108).

You must be on guard. Don't get taken.

Do not waste your life following the mystical claims of
miracles. Your best bet, with any disease, is to work with
educated, knowledgeable health professionals. That will
give you your best bet for health and survival. Perhaps you
could even volunteer to participate in medical research.

While you do that, you might become sensible in your
overall living. Although we do not know everything, there
are a lot of things that we do know about health. If your
cholesterol is too high, you should lower it. Ditto your blood
pressure. If you are too fat, lose weight. Do not smoke.

Regular aerobic exercise appears to improve the quality of your life. These and many more elements of your life style are totally within your control. They will help you to live a healthier and probably longer life.

Chapter 20

"Would You Like a Ride, Little Girl?"

One Is Too Many

Every parent would prefer to have his child grow up believing that the world is a wonderful, safe place. Today this fantasy is both unrealistic and dangerous. The fact is that children are being abducted and molested by strangers . . . everywhere. Boys as frequently as girls. But there comes a time when your child must be on his own, when you must let go. You can do so with relative confidence only if he is prepared to recognize and handle potentially dangerous situations.

Failure to prepare your child is foolish when the consequences are so enormous, so irrevocable. There is no valid excuse for withholding the knowledge and skills he needs to help short-circuit his own abduction, molestation or murder.

Never Say Yes to a Stranger (Newman 1985, 9).

You are well aware of the dangers your child can face when out of your sight. But does your child know? Have you taken the time to discuss it with him or her?

I am not talking about a one-time lesson giving instructions. I am talking about an ongoing dialogue.

Later in this book is a chapter entitled "NO! A Word That Can Save Your Life." Read that with your children. Take your time. Discuss it. Answer questions. Ask questions. Bring it up for discussion again at a later time.

That is just the beginning. There are some excellent books out there for children. They challenge your child to think and analyze. And, alas, there are some not-so-excellent books.

Some are very pat and simplistic. The answer to every situation given is something along the lines of "run away." While that is generally good, if it can be accomplished, it is not always possible, and it certainly is not always easy. The "run-away" type books do not write about a situation where an adult is physically restraining a child.

I particularly like *Never Say Yes to a Stranger* (Newman 1985). It presents true-to-life situations where the child has to use his or her wits. Each chapter concludes with an analysis of the choices. Then there is a list of things the child should know. And lastly, there is the "Always Remember" list. The book is an excellent learning tool, and an excellent springboard for your ongoing discussions with your child.

"Ongoing" is the key word in this. Reinforcement of the lessons is essential. Your child must have the necessary knowledge and understanding that will lead to the on-the-spot ability to think *and act*, in order to survive.

When should you start discussing this type of thing with your child? Today!

Chapter 21

Brainwashing: Broad and Narrow

Brainwashing: Broad Appeal

When you approached the old lady, you would use your most winning and pitiful look and tell her about your work for a Christian youth mission. The word Christian would win her. Never mind that Father [the cult leader] had said that Christians were worse than communists and that Satan was in them.

When you approached a young person, you would talk about the humanitarian goals of the Family [the cult]. Careful not to use the word "church."

Dark Side of the Moonies (Heftmann 1982, 94).

To get the flavor, picture yourself as a 21-year-old. It is late Friday afternoon. You have nothing, absolutely nothing, planned for the weekend. You are looking forward with dread to what promises to be an extremely lonely weekend.

You have just broken up with your girlfriend/boyfriend. You had gone together for two years. Your wedding date had been set for next June. And now it is all over.

OR

You just had a major fight with your parents. As you stormed out of the house, you told them that you would move out within five days.

OR

You have just been fired from work.

OR

Next week you will have final exams. Your are stressed out about that, especially in one course where you have not studied at all during the semester. Furthermore, you are not sure if you want to continue in the major subject you have selected for your degree.

OR

A dear friend has just died.

OR

Last Saturday you dropped an easy touchdown pass, thereby losing the conference championship for your university. You feel that you let your teammates, your coach, your friends, your family, and your school down.

In short, you are upset. No, "upset" is not strong enough —you are depressed on a grand scale.

As you are shuffling along, you come upon bright, sparkling, smiling people. They are about your age; the men are handsome and the women are beautiful. They are clean-scrubbed and clean-cut. They greet you warmly. "We're with the Feed the World's Children Crusade. Would you like to buy some flowers, or a book?"

You stop to chat with them. They tell you of a retreat to be held that weekend. As a matter of fact, they will be leaving for it at 6:30 p.m. They invite you to join them. They assure you that, "You are just the type of person we need for our Crusade. Please come. It's only for the weekend."

In further discussion you learn that, although everyone is serious about the Crusade, there will be singing and dancing. It will be fun.

Well, why not? In your current state of depression, what you most need is the supportive company of bright, attractive people. You will have just enough time to race home, pack some duds, and be on your way. Your parents will be out of town for the weekend. There is nobody who will know *or care* that you will be away for the weekend.

You thank them, and tell them you will be delighted to join them. They tell you where to meet the bus. You skip away with a new, surprising-to-you lightness and joy in your heart. Imagine, joining such fine people who are embarked on such a humanitarian venture, and to have fun while doing it.

At the weekend retreat, you are treated with respect and love. Warmth and love are all around you. There is much singing. Although there is preaching about God and the leader who runs the Crusade, it does not disturb you. After all, during the singing and preaching, you are holding hands with two very attractive members of the opposite sex.

Friday night is absolutely joyful. When you are awakened at 5:45 Saturday morning, you are not quite ready to start the day. But everybody else is up and moving, so you join them. Shortly, you are no longer thinking of your fatigue. Only the joy of the night just passed and the nobleness of your Crusade are on your mind.

I will spare you a description of the weekend. Your indoctrination into a religious cult is accepted by you without question. You were miserable before you joined, and now you are among dear friends. "Love-bombing" is one of the key tactics of the cults.

Sunday night comes too soon. The very dear friend with whom you have become intimate over the weekend invites you to stay just one more day. That, of course, will include one more night.

That is your moment of truth and moment of decision. If you decide to stay, you will probably have to make one telephone call. It may be to your parents, your employer, your school, or your girlfriend/boyfriend.

You make the call. Although you try to explain, you are greeted with, "What's the matter with you? Be responsible! Don't be a dummy! Leave wherever you are and come back to [me/home/school/work]."

As you hang up the telephone, depression has set in once more.

You are quickly greeted by a friendly, understanding voice, "See, we told you. They don't understand you out there. Stay with us. We need you. We love you. And, it appears that maybe you need us. You can build a life here. In addition to the loving atmosphere, you will be helping to feed the world's children. Please stay."

What do you do?

The above is one of many possible scenarios to indoctrinate you into a cult. Notice that, when you met them, they did not tell you of the cult/church to which they belonged. They have been instructed that, at that stage, you are not yet ready to know.

Contrary to popular opinion, it is not your overall personality and level of skepticism that determines whether you are susceptible to being lured into a cult. Rather, it is your mood and temperament at the particular moment that you are approached by cult members. The events in your life set out above would make you particularly vulnerable, regardless of your overall world view.

Please bear that in mind. It is a sad but true fact of life: You must always be on your guard.

✳ ✳ ✳ ✳ ✳ ✳
Brainwashing: Narrow Appeal

Sometimes a divorced mother will keep telling her child that his father hates him and that she is the only one who loves him, the only one he can trust. She may make the child think that his father is secretly his enemy and that he will be very cruel to him if he has the chance. Then when the child is alone with his father, and the father does something the child doesn't like, the child thinks this is proof that his father really hates him and that his mother is right.
The Boys and Girls Book About Divorce (Gardner 1970, 47).

When his wife Hzanke filed for divorce, Jim had enormous difficulty accepting the fact that his marriage was over. He still loved Hzanke, loved his children, and loved the family atmosphere. Finally, after a considerable amount of pain, he was able to come to terms with the break-up.

He was never able to come to terms with the fact that Hzanke told their children that their father did not love them, and that he had never loved them.

After the split, Hzanke denied Jim the right to see his children, notwithstanding explicit court orders which granted him the right. The domestic relations judge threatened to put her in jail if she continued to deny the father of her children the court-ordered visitation rights.

Once, on a specific court-ordered visitation date and time, Hzanke had her nine-year-old son call the police to report a strange man at the door. Hzanke was in the house at the time. She well knew it was her children's father at the door.

By agreement, the entire family went to an independent psychologist. His conclusions were:

- Jim was concerned about the welfare of his children, and felt personally deprived of his rights as a father.
- Hzanke was explicitly hostile toward Jim.

• The children sounded well-rehearsed and not spontaneous in their answers.

When the boys' bar mitzvah announcements appeared in the local paper, their father's name was conspicuously absent. This is virtually never done.

Another domestic relations judge observed in court, on the record, that Hzanke was poisoning the minds of the children against their father.

Hzanke had Jim arrested on criminal charges. She brought two of the children, ages ten and eight, into court to testify against their father. The facts of the case were substantially undisputed. The judge refused to allow the young children to testify against their father. He dismissed the case as being groundless.

All right: three judges and one psychologist went on the record pointing out Hzanke's hostility toward Jim. All observed the harmful effects on the children.

Sorry, dear readers, this story does not have a happy ending. The final judge in all such cases is, in fact, the children. These children have refused to speak with their father for, as of this writing, almost two decades.

As a point of information, mothers do not have a monopoly on brainwashing the children of divorce. Fathers do it too. Gender is not the distinguishing characteristic of parents who brainwash. Rather, the common characteristics are anger, cruelty, and stupidity.

If you cannot get along with your spouse and choose to separate, do not lay excessive burdens upon your children. Do not brainwash them. Although their father and mother cannot get along with each other, the children are still entitled to have both a mother and a father. Do not deprive them of this.

If you are a child of divorce, and if you have been told terrible things about one of your parents, find out for yourself whether it is true. Don't be taken in by the hostile and possibly false information given to you. Find out the facts. Seek out your estranged parent. You might confirm what you presently believe. On the other hand, you might be pleasantly surprised to find out that you are wrong, and that your parent really cares about you and loves you.

Regardless of the outcome of your quest, you will be better off. You will know the truth. Knowing the truth, even if it is unpleasant, has a way of cleansing your life and allowing you to come to terms with reality.

Find out!

Chapter 22

Communication With the Dead

I have never been baffled in the least by what I have seen at seances. Everything I have seen has been merely a form of mystification. The secret of all such performances is to catch the mind off guard and the moment after it has been surprised to follow up with something else that carries the intelligence along with the performer, even against the spectator's will.

> *Houdini—A Magician Among the Spirits*, by Harry Houdini, National President of The Society of American Magicians, 1917-1926 (Houdini [1924] 1972, 266).

Spook crooks is the name I have given fake spirit mediums, fortunetellers, and self-styled seers, who, through the practice of some material method, defraud the credulous and the superstitious. Claiming the special gifts of supersensitivity to the unseen, and the annihilation of both space and time, they offer the bereaved contact with the spirit world.

This predatory group picks up the secrets of magic, on the one hand, and imitates the effects recorded by the scientists as nearly as possible on the other, so that their "craft" is not even their own. Their only claim to authenticity is that they are genuine criminals.

The Dead Do Not Talk, by Julien J. Proskauer, National President of The Society of American Magicians, 1935-1936 (Proskauer 1946, xi and xvii).

Claimed communication with the dead is almost too grotesque to contemplate. However, contemplate it we must. The mystics sell it to bereaved family members of the deceased.

It is unconscionable that these bunco artists prey on bereavement, love, superstition, and human emotions to rob the bereaved of not only their money, but of the opportunity to come to terms with reality. By perpetrating the illusion that their customers can actually communicate with dead loved ones, the crime of fraud takes place in one of its most hateful settings.

There is *no reliable evidence*—NONE, not the slightest shred—that living humans can communicate with the dead. That holds true for spiritualism, channeling, and any of the myriad other names used for this abhorrent act by the heinous perpetrators of this bunco.

Death of a loved one is a horror without equal. But, if you are to survive as a functioning human being, you must come to terms with the reality of what has happened.

Don't get taken. Do not believe things that fly in the face of everything you know and believe. Do not let hope and wishes interfere with your good, common sense. Trust your common sense over the glowing lies of the con artists, no matter how strongly you might *wish* that what they say could possibly be true.

Chapter 23

Belief in Mystics Can Be Dangerous to Your Wealth, Health, and Life

Gee, Bob, why are you so hard on psychics? What's the problem if people choose to believe? Isn't it just a harmless diversion?
A line of questioning frequently directed at me.

At the conclusion of my exclusive magical performance for an audience of two, both mother and daughter applauded. For the daughter, it was painful for her to do so.

She was nine years old, and was dying of cancer. She had lost all power of speech and most of her mobility. She was in pain 24 hours of every day. Her mind was still active and alert.

A psychic telephoned her mother to tell her that the reason her child was dying of cancer was because the mother had had marital problems while she was pregnant. He went on to assure the mother that if she consulted him, he could reverse the process.

Many parents in that case would have run to the psychic, and would have thrown money at him.

The child died three weeks after I met her. If the mother had been a believer, she would have lived not only with the horror that her nine-year-old child had died painfully of cancer, but also would have had to live with the life-long guilt that somehow it was her fault.

No, friends, belief in psychics is not some innocent, harmless diversion.

In this book you have read some of the horrors resulting from such belief.

Many people are convinced that their own belief level is limited. They read the daily astrology column in the newspaper "just for fun." They may even follow the advice, if it is just a minor inconvenience. For example, the column may advise not to make any business deals that morning, but rather to wait until the afternoon. The reader will then call a business associate to reschedule the luncheon appointment from 11:30 a.m. to noon.

That seemingly minor disruption of schedule can become a pattern. Then, when real problems come, and when a money-grubbing mystic is on hand offering to advise you, what do you do?

Do not get trapped into even starting to believe, even to some minor, seemingly silly degree, in bunkum. It can hurt you. It has hurt many. Keep your mind firmly planted in reality. It will lead to a happier, freer life.

PART V

HOW TO PROTECT YOURSELF AND THOSE YOU LOVE AGAINST BUNCO AND BUNKUM

Chapter 24

Why Bunco and Bunkum Flourish

I urge my readers to beware of quacks and phonies. I warn them against the charlatans and fakers. More often than I care to admit, I have received in return a seething reply: "How dare you take away our hope! I'll bet you are on the payroll of the American Medical Association. The medical doctor didn't do anything but send us big bills. Jesus Christ is the greatest healer of them all. Now that we have put our child in His hands, we know everything is going to be all right."
    The Ann Landers Encyclopedia (Landers 1978, 994).

Those who sell bunco (fraud) are thieving con artists. They plan, scheme, calculate, and analyze how to take your money. Their goal is to make you dependent upon them. They want you to need them and their product or service.

Having read this far, I trust and sincerely hope that you are ready for the next paragraph.

Those who sell bunkum (nonsense) are frequently sincere. They truly believe that their product or service will help you. With that belief in mind, they plan, scheme, calculate, and analyze how to take your money. Their goal is to make you dependent upon them. They want you to need them and their product or service.

All of us wish that there might be simple answers to our complex problems. All of us were told fairy tales when we were children. In them, the good people always win, often magically.

Whether we like it or not, real life functions in reality. There are not magical answers. That clear fact does not stop people from wishing for magical answers to life's complex problems. Nor does it stop them from paying for those magical answers.

If you would simply stop to think about many of the claimed miraculous income sources and medical treatments offered, that alone would often be enough to save you from being taken. The same goes for the claimed mystical peeks into the future.

Those who try to inform the public are often chastised for doing so. Ann Landers has had an excellent newspaper advice column for decades. The quotation at the top of this chapter shows the reaction she frequently gets for her sage advice.

I have often been in similar circumstances. When I appear on television with a psychic, those who believe that I am correct say, "Nice going, Bob." Beyond that, they do not need me.

Those who believe that the psychic is correct follow her home and throw money at her. They believe that they need her advice to guide their lives.

The purveyors of these scams and nonsense are not prosecuted often enough. The convictions are far too low. Often they will get a sentence that is nothing more than a "slap on the wrist." A man was recently convicted in California of being a psychic surgeon. He plea bargained and got only a nine-month jail sentence.

People who are taken are often embarrassed and ashamed. Many believe they have been a party to an illegal transaction. That last belief may not line up with the facts, but the mark will not learn that until *after* the crime is reported to the police. Many cons purposely convince the mark that he/she is buying stolen goods, failing to report found money, or other such things. These and other reasons cause the person to not report the crime to the police. When they do report it, frequently they wait too long to do so.

The public—all of us—must rethink the way we view con artists and bunkum salespeople.

The bunco sellers are thieves, crooks, and anti-social destroyers of the fabric of civilized society. The sincere bunkum sellers, although not thieves, are also destroyers of the fabric of civilized society.

We *must* get in the habit of calling the police at the first hint, at the first suspicion, that a con game or misrepresentation may be operating. Do not wait until the trail gets cold.

If you take action and call the police, you will be protecting the rest of us. You will also be helping to protect yourself and your loved ones. The protection from and apprehension of criminals is one of the very important functions of society. To make it work, we all must participate.

We must also express our outrage that con artists are frequently not prosecuted. For reasons that no government prosecuting attorney has ever explained to me, con artists, phony medical hucksters, and mystics often do not run into serious problems with the law. If there is a political message in this book—and there is—it is this:

We must turn around the lackadaisical attitude that the general public and some parts of law enforcement have toward con artists and misrepresenters.

The purveyors of bunco are criminals.

The sincere sellers of bunkum, although generally not technically considered to be criminals, destroy much of what is good in society.

The policeman and policewoman who put their lives on the line every day are the real heroes.

The selling of fraud and misrepresentation must be stopped.

If there is a purpose in having a government—and I believe that there is—it is for the protection of individual rights.

We must aid and encourage our law enforcement people to apprehend, prosecute, and convict those who spend their lives ripping off the money and ripping up the self-esteem, emotions, and the health of honest people.

Life functions based upon reality, taking into account *all* the people who enter your life. Some of them, albeit a minority, will try to cheat you. If you understand that, and if you are prepared for that, in the long run you will be far happier.

There is a necessary postscript to this chapter, lest you even consider being lured into what may, at first blush, appear to be a glamorous life of crime. The following can be confirmed by virtually any law enforcement professional, psychologist, or sociologist, as well as by observing and by reading the case studies.

Although it may not be apparent on the surface, the purveyors of bunco and bunkum are in fact losers. They are the dregs of life. They have contempt for their fellow human beings. And, sooner or later, their fellow human beings will end up hating those who have taken them.

Many, probably most, of the grifters and misrepresenters end up broke and lonely. They spend their lives as drifters. The short-term lure of money and glamour fade. They cannot hold on to either the money or the glamour.

It is difficult, by logic, to explain why. It does not seem to make sense. However, applying our present knowledge of the psychology of human beings, it makes a great deal of sense. These deceiving, conniving sellers of bunco and bunkum are hateful people and, evidently, end up doing to themselves what they have done to others.

It is well-nigh impossible for those people to have loving family or friends. I am talking about *real* love and *real* friends. Never will they find contentment.

They cannot love, and cannot receive a healthy love. They cannot be true friends to anybody. As near as I can figure out, having discussed this with psychologists, the con artists are psychopaths. They seem to be without consciences, and without compassion for their fellow human beings. They are lonely, and can never achieve what most of us need—a shared warmth with other human beings.

Chapter 25

Does It Make Sense?

The more umpossible a thing is, the more we stand in feare thereof; and the lesse likelie to be true, the more we beleeve it. And if we were not such, I thinke . . . that these divinors, astrologers, conjurors, and cousenors [frauds] would die for hunger.
The Discoverie of Witchcraft (Scot [1584] 1972, 121).

Goode folke, an [if] I did wish, 'twould be easie for me to translate the above into moderne English. Howe'er, I bethinke me 'twould be fun for ye to trie to understand it as 'twas writ by Reginald Scot in 1584.

Take the time to think about what is being sold to you. Many of the sales pitches simply do not make sense. As stated before, for many of the cons and nonsense it does not require any specialized knowledge on your part. All that is required is for you to use your good common sense.

Let us look at some examples.

The foundation of astrology is that the "sign" you were born under influences your personality. Think about that.

The "signs" come from the musings of our ancestors looking up at the sky several thousand years ago. They tried to make sense of their universe. They perceived pictures formed by the stars. For example, one group of stars looked like a lion. They would draw pictures of the formations on the caves in which they lived.

We call these formations *constellations*.

Later, when astrology was founded, names were attached to the pictures assigned to the constellations. Thus, we have Leo the Lion as one of the signs of the zodiac.

From earth, we perceive the formation of the constellation Leo the Lion. However, the stars making that up are millions of light years apart. Looked at from another part of the universe, you would not see that constellation.

All of the stars in that constellation are light years from earth.

Now think about this. How likely is it that the cave people's perception of stars which are light years apart could have an influence on your personality for all of your life?

Look at sun-sign astrology. How likely is it that you share the same personality with one-twelfth of the population of the earth? How about the idea that every single person with whom you share your personality was born within one month of you? And, if you buy this nonsense, you do not have a personality similar to any of the eleven-twelfths of the people who were born under any other sign.

Now, really, isn't all of that just plain silly?

✳ ✳ ✳ ✳ ✳ ✳

Many people work very hard all of their lives to support themselves and their families. Then you receive in the mail a pyramid scheme which informs you that, with little effort, you can earn $50,000 any time you want. With ease, so you are told, you can become a millionaire.

Isn't that just a silly fairy tale? Well, yes, it is—but only if you take the time to think about it, and to apply it to the test of your common sense.

✻ ✻ ✻ ✻ ✻ ✻

Ah, yes, the all-time favorite of the con artists is the pigeon drop. Someone whom you have known for a period of only ten minutes wants to share with you one-third of the $12,000 which she found. Aren't you lucky?

Does that make any sense?

Stop to think about it. If you did, you would *never* put up "good faith" money in cash to show a complete stranger that you are honorable.

✻ ✻ ✻ ✻ ✻ ✻

The blood readers would narrow your personality groups down to only four. It has the same objections as does astrology. If you would only take the time to think about it, you would realize that it is bunkum.

✻ ✻ ✻ ✻ ✻ ✻

Faith healing, psychic surgery, and other claimed medical miracles claim the money of millions of people, and the lives of far too many.

Does it make any sense that a theatrical preacher can cure you without even making a clear medical analysis and diagnosis of your condition?

Does it make sense that someone can perform an operation and remove a diseased tumor from inside your body without making an incision?

Scientists, millionaires, presidents of countries, kings and queens, Nobel laureates, and physicians themselves seek the services of physicians when they are sick.

Does it make any sense that you can do it more easily and more cheaply, and with no physical pain whatsoever, *regardless of your illness*?

If you take the time to think and to apply your common sense to this highly emotional situation, I am sure you will realize that those claimed miracles are grotesque fraud.

❋ ❋ ❋ ❋ ❋ ❋

Millionaires, government leaders, business leaders, union leaders, CPAs, attorneys, financial planners, and others file income tax returns. Often they pay substantial sums in income tax. Additionally, they may pay professional fees to CPAs, attorneys, or other tax advisors to assist them in the analysis and preparation of their tax returns.

For $10.95, you can purchase Irwin Schiff's *How Anyone Can Stop Paying Income Taxes* (Schiff and Murzin 1982), in which you are clearly told that you legally do not have to file income tax returns, and that legally you do not have to pay income taxes.

A moment's reflection will tell you that Schiff's advice flies in the face of common sense.

❋ ❋ ❋ ❋ ❋ ❋

Does it cure everything?

Suppose I told you that I could manipulate your . . . you fill in the part of the body you wish: feet, hands, back, head, you name it . . . and cure everything that could possibly ail you.

Suppose I told you that taking a certain dosage of a certain vitamin would prevent everything from cancer and heart attack to the common cold.

There are people out there telling the world those very things. They are selling their products and services.

Anyone who has one procedure which is claimed to prevent and/or cure every imaginable disease is a quack. That is true whether the person is sincere or a con artist.

✳ ✳ ✳ ✳ ✳ ✳

The future does not now exist. It will be created as a result of the actions of every living and non-living thing in the universe. That means not only human beings, but animals, insects, trees, wind, hurricanes, tornadoes, earthquakes, and more.

If I decide to stay home all day tomorrow, you will not be able to meet me on Main Street at noon.

With all of these interactions, does it seem possible that some human being could actually sort them out and accurately predict the future? It does not make any sense. It is not even remotely possible.

✳ ✳ ✳ ✳ ✳ ✳

Take the time to apply your good common sense to whatever happens in your life. It will protect you and those you love from most of the bunco and bunkum that comes your way.

Anything that flies in the face of common sense is not something you want to rush to buy or invest in. Nor do you want to believe in it.

Chapter 26

Take Your Time

Time and patience are power.
Give & Take: The Complete Guide to Negotiating Strategies
and Tactics (Karrass 1974, 154).

Does it seem strange to you that I am quoting from a book on negotiating to get across a point on how to protect yourself against bunco and bunkum?

In all business deals, in fact in all transactions in life, there is an element of negotiation. Any time you allow yourself to be rushed and hustled into a decision, you run the odds-on risk that you will be hurt. This goes in spades when you are dealing with a con artist.

But how do you know if you are dealing with a con artist? You do not—until you take the time to think about what is going on. Then you will be in a far better position to make an informed judgment on that score. As a matter of fact, taking the time to think will put you in a far better position to evaluate and act on *any* course of action offered to you: honest or crooked, business or personal.

The act of taking your time until you are ready for a decision applies to virtually all transactions. It is almost never a good idea to allow yourself to be rushed into a decision before you have had time to think about it. I say "almost never," because there are indeed times when I would act instantly, and could justify my actions. For example, if I heard guns being fired in the street, and a policeman were to advise me to duck behind a tree before I got killed, I would do so—most immediately and most obediently. However, even that action on my part would not be without thinking. A quick evaluation of the circumstances would lead me to conclude that:

- with gunshots being fired, I would probably be safer behind a tree than out in the open, and

- since the man is dressed as a policeman, and since the advice he gave me is obviously quite sensible, it is probably a good idea for me to trust him.

Taking your time will allow you to discuss the venture with others: your business associates, family, friends, and perhaps even professional advisors. For example, on a business investment, you might wish to consult an attorney, CPA, or other financial advisor. In any event, allow yourself the time to gather the necessary information to make an informed decision.

There is an interesting fringe benefit to taking your time. Honest business people will not object if you wish to think about a proposition for a reasonable amount of time. Con artists get extremely upset if you delay at all. They may even run away from you!

For *any* new deal or new concept in our lives, we all need to allow ourselves the time to get used to it. Do not be rushed or hustled.

Many people who are taken are not even aware of it. They allow themselves to be hustled and conned.

You purchase merchandise worth $3.23, and hand the clerk a $20.00 bill. You receive change of $6.77 (that is, change as if you had paid $10.00). If you walk away, the transaction is over—you lost $10.00. If you mention it, the clerk merely responds, "Oops. Sorry," and hands you another $10.00. It is very difficult to build a criminal case against such people—one that will stand up in court. Suppose only one person in 10 walks away. The clerk still makes a healthy profit on the theft.

Short-change artists can be on either side of the counter. Some of the slick *flimflam* [deception] would stagger your senses. Suppose you are behind the counter, giving change of a $20.00 for a purchase of $6.83. The customer puts up four additional dollars and asks for two ten-dollar bills in the change. Whoa! Slow down! Your protection is to complete one transaction, put the money away, and then to address the next request. Otherwise, you will lose money. It will take you until three minutes after he leaves to sort out in your mind what happened.

Switches of your billfold or attaché case can take place in a moment of inattention on your part, while the con artist is fast-talking you on another matter.

Take your time. If you detect an undue sense of urgency on the part of someone you are thinking about dealing with, run, do not walk, away.

Chapter 27

Other Considerations

I never invest in anything I don't know anything about.
Ed Cottingham, in a conversation.

While the above statement might seem obvious, it is in fact quite profound. Any of us might casually make that statement. However, when presented with a lucrative opportunity to make a lot of money in a new, unfamiliar venture, many people would jump at it. Many people have jumped at it, and have been taken badly, for a lot of money.

Cottingham's statement was not an off-hand comment that he threw out casually. Throughout his life he has, as have most of us, been offered many seemingly golden opportunities. His was a statement of philosophy, an absolute guideline to which he has steadfastly adhered.

Some things require specialized knowledge. Smart as you might be generally, you should not invest in a business that claims to be selling quarks to local grammar schools. Knowledge of what quarks are is a prerequisite to any financial investment in them.

It takes a considerable amount of guts and a high level of self-esteem to simply say, "That is not for me. I know nothing about it. I will stay away. No, thank you."

It is necessary for you to do that. Many people have gone into honest, potentially lucrative business ventures in fields with which they were unfamiliar, and about which they did an inadequate amount of study and preparation. It should come as no surprise to you that they lost. Honest or crooked, if you invest in unfamiliar fields, you are bound to lose.

❄ ❄ ❄ ❄ ❄ ❄

Is it too good to be true?

If something sounds as if it is too good to be true, it is probably just that: it is too good to be true. Ergo, it is not true.

Exercise extreme caution in such circumstances. And do not rush.

❄ ❄ ❄ ❄ ❄ ❄

The burden of proof.

The astrologers claim that the planets and stars influence your life and personality. Suppose an astrologer challenges you to disprove it. When you are unable to do so, he proudly proclaims that his case is proven.

There is a fundamental scientific principle at issue. The one who makes the claim has the burden of proof. Let us illustrate that principle with a silly but nonetheless important example.

Suppose I tell you that I can flap my arms and fly. I use no motors. I do it under my own power.

Do you believe it? No. Can you prove that I cannot do it? No, again.

Then I say, "Well, I can't prove it, and you can't disprove it. It's a toss-up. We will have to suspend judgment on it. Meanwhile, unless you want to lose out on the benefits, you might as well act as if it is true. What can you lose?"

Do you buy that? No, of course not.

I claimed that I can fly. Unless and until I present convincing evidence of that ability, you have nothing to disprove. I made the claim. Therefore, the burden of proof is on me.

Back to the stars. The astrologer will then accuse you of having a closed mind, and of being narrow-minded.

That is not the case. If he were to present proof of his claim, would you be willing to evaluate it? Yes, of course you would. If his proof warranted belief, would you be willing to reevaluate your present thinking? Yes, again.

Good! You have an open mind. You are receptive to new ideas. However, that does *not* mean that you will automatically believe everything anybody tells you. Unless and until that claimant presents good evidence to support his claim, there is nothing for you to do or to believe in.

The same holds true for bending a spoon with the mind, reincarnation, remote viewing, channeling, and every other scientific claim.

The burden of proof is on the one making the claim.

❋ ❋ ❋ ❋ ❋ ❋

When you seek an explanation for something, unless there is convincing evidence to the contrary, tentatively accept the most reasonable answer. This is variously known in science as *Occam's razor* (named after the fourteenth century English philosopher, William of Occam: assumptions introduced to explain something must not be unnecessarily multiplied) or *parsimony* (economy of explanation; this is generally related to Occam's razor).

Let us take an example. Psychic Uri Geller claims that he can bend a spoon or key by using psychic powers. We know as an absolute certainty that there are thousands of magicians who can create the exact same illusion by normal means, using trickery. Decide which explanation you consider to be more reasonable, and hence more likely to be the correct explanation:

- The human being named Uri Geller has the supernatural powers to violate the known laws of nature at his whim.

OR

- Uri Geller has learned the same trick that thousands of magicians have learned. He is a normal human being, and does things by normal means.

When it is put that way, it is easy, isn't it?

❋ ❋ ❋ ❋ ❋ ❋

Trust me.

It is important, perhaps even essential, to trust the people you deal with. That is true on both the business and personal levels.

However, consider it to be a danger signal when your display of trust in the other person is the sole issue for consideration. If the person unreasonably demands unquestioning trust, watch out.

Why are you asking all those detailed, pesky questions? The numbers get complicated. Doing that financial analysis would just waste our time. What's the matter—don't you trust me?

Of course the new blacktop job we did on your driveway will last. It is guaranteed for a year. You don't need it in writing. My word is my bond. Would I lie to you?

>   You don't need a receipt for the cash you gave me. Trust
>   me!
>
>   You're kidding! Do you really want to run this by your
>   lawyer and CPA before you sign? Do you think I would
>   try to pull a fast one? Come on!
>
>   Let's let this loan be our secret. Of course I'll pay you
>   back. But I don't want my spouse to know, so I'd rather
>   not sign any papers.

As the gambler said: "I trust everybody, but I always cut the deck."

Protect yourself in your negotiations and contracts. If you do, everybody wins, except the con artist.

❋ ❋ ❋ ❋ ❋ ❋

Falsifiability.

Back to science. It is important to understand some fundamental concepts.

The principle of falsifiability was introduced by Karl R. Popper, Austrian philosopher and economist. Suppose I assert that something is true. In order for my statement to be a scientific claim, there must be some way, at least in theory, to prove that it is false. A few examples will serve to illustrate the point.

>   I claim that water is made of two parts of hydrogen and
>   one part of oxygen. You can test it. You mix two parts
>   of hydrogen and one part of oxygen. If you get water,
>   my scientific claim is correct. If you do not get water,
>   my scientific claim is incorrect—you have falsified it.
>   In either case, it is a scientific claim. It is capable of
>   being falsified.
>
>   I claim that the world is flat. I have staked my claim: I
>   claim that the world is flat, while simultaneously claim-
>   ing that it is not non-flat. You can test it. By flying
>   around the world in an airplane, you have falsified my
>   claim. It is, nonetheless, a scientific claim.

An astrologer held forth on the value of sun signs in predicting your personality. I challenged her to guess my sun sign. She kept guessing and kept missing. After eleven misses, she finally guessed on the twelfth guess (there are twelve signs). She instantly started explaining that sun signs are meaningless. It is moon signs that are important. Hers was *not* a scientific claim. She would not allow it to be falsified. After her original claim was falsified, she slid to a new position. She did not hold to her claim.

Unless there is something, at least in theory, that can falsify a claim, you do not have a scientific claim.

Think of this when some mystic wants you to buy his or her claim. Think about whether it is scientific.

❈ ❈ ❈ ❈ ❈ ❈

Whether a claim has been scientifically tested and validated is important. The proponents of laetrile brought forth a lot of testimonials. But they lacked good scientific evidence. That should put you on notice that there is nothing to count on. They do not have a claim that has been proven to be safe and effective.

❈ ❈ ❈ ❈ ❈ ❈

Sometimes you can analyze a claim or offer from several different points of view. If all of them lead you to the conclusion that it is bunkum, then you may rest secure that it is indeed bunkum.

Let us apply this to the claimed ability to see into the future.

As we saw in Chapter 25, the idea that someone could actually foretell the future is clearly nonsense. Let us delve deeper.

The idea is too good to be true. Think about it. Most of the world struggles, plans, and works to secure a happy future. Now here is a mystic who tells you that, for money, he or she can look ahead to a time that has not yet come.

Unlike everybody else, you will not have to work to secure your future. The mystic will tell you.

Fortune-telling has not been scientifically validated. The tests would be simple: record the predictions and see if they come true. No validation by this simple procedure under proper scientific conditions has ever been demonstrated by the mystics. Fortune-telling has not been scientifically validated.

How does the burden of proof apply to fortune-telling? The mystics offer no proof. Therefore, from that standpoint, you have no reason to believe in it.

Let us consider Occam's razor, or parsimony. Decide which you consider more likely:

- Someone can actually sort out the infinite number of interactions among people, animals, and things, and is able to *know* the outcome and can predict the future.

OR

- The mystic is faking it.

I prefer the latter explanation. It is far more reasonable.

Therefore, you are left with your trust—actually blind faith—in the mystic as the *only* basis for making a favorable judgment on fortune-telling.

All roads lead clearly and inescapably to the conclusion that fortune-telling is pure bunkum.

✳ ✳ ✳ ✳ ✳ ✳

Is the person sincere?

As we have seen, the fact that a person is sincere does not make that person correct. Sincerity alone is not enough; validity and correctness are essential before you spend your time and money on something offered to you.

✳ ✳ ✳ ✳ ✳ ✳

How do you decide what to believe?

The mystical claims have not been validated by science. Many of the sellers of phony medical claims do not even claim scientific validation. Those that do are frequently either lying or in error. Many of the mystical and street-scam claims are illogical. Much of the bunkum only requires that you use your good common sense to see that it is nonsense.

If something has not been validated by science, if it is illogical, and if it flies in the face of common sense, there is no reason for you to believe in it. There is certainly no reason for you to pay for it.

Do not believe in something because it would be nice if it were so. Otherwise, we adults would all go through life believing in Santa Claus.

There comes a time to leave Santa Claus behind. There comes a time to deal with reality, face to face. You will be far happier, healthier, and wealthier for deciding to do so.

Chapter 28

NO! A Word That Can Save Your Life

(Read this with your children.)

When you yell, shout things such as "You don't know me!" "I'm being kidnapped!" "You're not my father!" so people will realize that you are not having a fight with your parent. You want everyone around to know that you are not having a temper tantrum either, that a stranger is trying to take you against your will.

Never Say Yes to a Stranger (Newman 1985, 65).

Most people in the world are nice and can be trusted. But that is not true of all people.

Some people will try to hurt you. They will try to take you away from your home.

You cannot judge whether you can trust someone by looking at him or her. The person may look very nice and friendly. But there may be trouble.

Learn to say "NO!"

If a stranger approaches you *for any reason*, get away. You do not have to be nice to a stranger.

Someone you just met may offer you a ride home from school, or ice cream, or a baby kitten. The answer must always be "No." (If you like, you may try "No, thank you.")

The person may argue with you. He or she may say that you are unfair, or that you are not being nice. Often such a person will try to make you feel guilty, saying such things as: "Trust me! You look like a big boy/girl. Why are you acting like a baby? Come on, get into my car." Do not believe that.

After you try "No, thank you," then just get away. Just run away.

Never go into anyone's home or car without permission from your parents.

People may try to hurt you. They may try to touch private parts of your body. They do not have the right to do that.

They may want you to take drugs. The answer is "NO!"

If ever there is any trouble, get to a telephone and call the police. They will help you. The police are on your side.

Children always count on their parents or relatives to protect them. But, your first and last line of defense is you. Your parents cannot always be with you.

When you are walking home from school, and an adult in a car offers you a ride, candy, or makes any other approach, you must get away. At that time, your parents, the police, and all the laws in the world cannot protect you. You must protect yourself! Once more: Your first and last line of defense is you.

Your very survival depends upon knowing what to do at the time a stranger approaches you. Drugs can be very dangerous. Talking with strangers is very dangerous. Going for a ride with a stranger is very dangerous.

It would be nice if everyone in the world were nice. But that is not the case.

"NO!" is a word that can save your life.

Let's talk about drugs for a little bit.

Some drugs, prescribed by your doctor and approved by your parents, can be very helpful.

Other drugs, the type you may have seen being passed around at your school, are extremely dangerous. It is a shame to have to scare you, but I must tell you: Drugs can kill you! Please understand that: Drugs can kill you!

Classmates you thought were friends may try to get you to take drugs. They may call you "chicken" or "coward." They are not your friends! They are not being nice to you! The answer is "NO!"

Do not experiment. Do not sample.

There are so many wonderful things to do in life. Magic is a wonderful hobby. Baseball is wonderful. Piano playing is fun. There are just so many good things to do.

One of the best things you can do for yourself is to learn a lot. Listen in school. Do your homework. Do more than just get by. Really learn what is being taught. Learn new things.

When you pay attention in school, you may well find that what your teachers are teaching you is very interesting. It is fun to learn.

Read. Reading can be an adventure that can stay with you all your life.

Learning is exciting.

You may try any or all of the good things to do.

But if you try drugs, they may blot out your mind. You may not be able to think. Then you will not be able to do any of the very many fun things in life.

Happiness and joy in life come when you are alert and aware, and when you are ready to enjoy being alive. If you take drugs, you will not be able to enjoy many of the pleasures in life.

Remember: Stay away from strangers. Do not go with strangers. Always let your parents know where you are. Get their permission to do things.

If anyone tells you there is something that you cannot tell your parents, that is a signal. You *must* tell your parents that thing.

Let's say you are in a shopping mall with your mother. You wander away. A strange man tries to take you away. You start to get away from him. He grabs your arm. What do you do?

Start yelling. Read again the quote at the top of the chapter. Read it over and over, so that if you ever need it, you will know the type of thing to yell.

That will get the attention of other people.

Never accept that you must go with a stranger. Keep alert. Keep thinking. Try to think of ways to get away.

Here is an important game you can play. Think of situations where you really would not know what to do. Imagine how you would protect yourself and how you would get away. Discuss these situations with your parents, brothers and sisters, teachers, and classmates. It is amazing how much we can learn in life by discussing things with trusted people. Encourage your friends to try to think of problems. Then you try, along with them, to think of the best way to handle the situations.

Now that you have read this chapter, think about it. Discuss it with your parents. Talk to your brothers and sisters about it. Talk to your friends about it. Bring it up in school: talk to your teachers and classmates.

Discussing this with your family, teachers, and trusted friends will reinforce the lessons that you must learn.

Always remember the word "NO!" One last time: "NO!" is a word that can save your life!

Chapter 29

A Final Word

No police force or medical society in the world has the power to stop people from preying upon our gullibility. Your only defense is a little skepticism, especially when the evidence is beyond belief.
Dean Edell, M.D. (Edell 1989).

Your first and last line of defense is you. Dr. Dean Edell has said it. I have said it. Others have said it. Now you must say it. You must believe it.

The police have done and are doing a wonderful job in tracking down bunco artists. Increasingly, law enforcement agencies are engaged in crime prevention, in giving educational presentations to the public. It is far better to have an informed citizenry and to prevent a crime, than to have to apprehend a criminal after the devastation is done to the innocent.

The skeptics have done and are doing an increasingly good job of educating the public about both bunco and bunkum in the mystical field. Scientists are coming around, sometimes grudgingly, to the realization and acceptance that they must dispel the nonsense in the public mind if science is to continue to advance at its best possible rate.

Magicians have taken on an increased civic responsibility in educating the public, as well as in overseeing scientific experiments, in order to eliminate trickery. In designing a test for claimed psychic ability, many scientists now recognize the need to have magicians who are trained in psychic investigation on hand.

Educators are giving more attention to enlightening their students about critical thinking. We all had teachers who challenged us to think. And, alas, we also had some teachers who simply drummed a bunch of facts into our heads. Our job, and our grade in the course, depended upon our accepting *uncritically* the information force-fed to us, and feeding it back on the final exam.

Think back—the teachers whom you most liked, the ones who stand out in your mind, the ones who made learning exciting—which ones were they? I'll give you eight to five they were the ones who encouraged critical thinking.

And now, what about you? Do you want to be dependent upon others who profess a pipeline to mystical information, or who claim to have a fast-buck scheme that will make you a millionaire within a year?

No! Don't get taken! Do not let yourself be intimidated by their name-calling and insults. You are the owner of your own life. When you shed your wishful ways and stop waiting for the miracles of a fortune-teller or quick-money scam, you will have more control over your own life. With that will come increased self-esteem.

Attend and participate in public awareness presentations. Continue to seek knowledge in reading and from trusted sources. Think about what you read in this book.

Think back to it now and then. Discuss these matters with trusted friends.

As you address the real world, do not follow the pie-in-the-sky promises of claims that are, literally, too good to be true. You will find that you will be more successful in every area of your life. And you will be happier.

The final word: We thank all of the wonderful people who are doing things to prevent bunco and bunkum. We appreciate the educators *in all fields* who are increasing public awareness of the risks. With all due respects to all of them, when it comes to protecting yourself against the ravages of bunco and bunkum, your first and last line of defense is *YOU*! Remain aware and alert.

DON'T GET TAKEN!

EPILOGUE

The Final Exam

I hope you found this book both interesting and informative.

I know that I have gained from my study of the subject. On Friday morning, July 7, 1989, at about 2:15 a.m., I field-tested my knowledge—in the streets—and not by choice.

The book was done. After a few finishing touches, it would be ready for printing.

I took off to attend a magic convention, where I would be giving a presentation. One evening, at about 2:00 a.m., we called it a night. The warm, friendly conversation ended. I started walking back to my hotel, alone.

A large man called to me from across the street. I realized that I had let my guard down. I had not observed the rules that I know so well. The streets were dark. There was no one else around. I was tired. I was slouching and shuffling along in my walk. I was reasonably well dressed, and was carrying a shopping bag (filled with wondrous magic I had just bought).

Realizing that the above was the classic invitation to a street thief, I instantly changed my entire bearing. I straightened up to my full height and started to walk briskly. That, plus ignoring the person, is the textbook way to handle a stranger in streets. Usually the stranger will just move on.

That approach did not work. He started to follow me, while he continued to talk to me. (I later learned that the textbook approach generally does not work in that city: The panhandlers are much more aggressive and tend to be violent.)

I quickened my pace. He quickened his pace. He was gaining on me.

I looked in all directions—darkness was everywhere. He called out, "You ain't gonna get away, man!" He kept walking and kept talking.

As I started to walk even faster, I desperately considered my options:

- Could I outrun him? Probably not. Could I outfight him? Most assuredly not. He earns his livelihood in the streets. Isn't there *anything* I can do? If he beats me up, it will delay publication of the book.

- Aha! The book! That was the spark of inspiration. If I am an expert at anything in the streets, it is the con game. To pull it off, I would have to use the language of the streets.

I stopped, turned to face him squarely, and said firmly and confidently, "Look, buddy, I got no time to mess with you. I'm on a very important case. If you make me stop to bust you . . . if you make me miss out on arresting the guy I've been tracking, I'll throw the f_____ book at you!"

He stopped dead in his tracks, paused for a moment, then turned and walked away.

*BIBLIOGRAPY
AND
RESOURCES*

BIBLIOGRAPHY

Abell, George O. and Barry Singer, Editors. 1981. *Science and the Paranormal*. New York: Charles Scribner's Sons.

Amyx, Meredy. 1988. "Nothing Up My Sleeve." *Mensa Bulletin*. October 1988. Brooklyn: American Mensa, Ltd.

Anderson, Walter. 1986. *Courage is a Three-Letter Word*. New York: Fawcett Crest.

Auerbach, Loyd. 1986. *ESP, Hauntings and Poltergeists: A Parapsychologist's Handbook*. New York: Warner Books.

Bank of America. 1987. *For Our Customers*. San Francisco: Bank of America.

Barrett, Stephen, M.D., Editor. 1980. *The Health Robbers*. Philadelphia: George F. Stickley Company.

Bok, Bart J. and Lawrence E. Jerome. 1975. *Objections to Astrology*. Buffalo: Prometheus Books.

Bowyer, J. Barton. 1982. *Cheating*. New York: St. Martin's Press.

Carey, Mary and George Sherman. 1976. *A Compendium of Bunk or How to Spot a Con Artist*. Springfield, IL: Charles C. Thomas.

Christopher, Milbourne. 1970. *ESP, Seers & Psychics*. New York: Thomas Y. Crowell Company.

————-. 1975. *Mediums, Mystics & the Occult*. New York: Thomas Y. Crowell Company.

Consumer Reports Books, Editors of. 1980. *Health Quackery*. New York: Holt, Rinehart and Winston.

CSICOP—The Committee for the Scientific Investigation of Claims of the Paranormal. Quarterly. *The Skeptical Inquirer*. Buffalo: CSICOP.

Culver, R. B. and P. A. Ianna. [1979] 1984. *The Gemini Syndrome: A Scientific Evaluation of Astrology*. Buffalo: Prometheus Books.

Edell, Dean, M.D. 1989. "Beyond Belief." *Channel 7 News at 11:00*. May 1989. San Francisco: KGO Channel 7 News.

Evans, Christopher. 1973. *Cults of Unreason*. New York: Farrar, Straus and Giroux.

Gardner, Martin. 1981. *Science—Good, Bad and Bogus*. Buffalo: Prometheus Books.

Gardner, Richard A., M.D. 1970. *The Boys and Girls Book About Divorce*. New York: Bantam Books.

Gauquelin, Michel. 1979. *Dreams and Illusions of Astrology*. Buffalo: Prometheus Books.

Gibson, Walter B. 1946. *The Bunco Book*. Holyoke, MA: Sidney H. Radner.

Goodman, Linda. 1968. *Linda Goodman's Sun Signs*. New York: Bantam Books.

Gordon, Henry. 1987. *ExtraSensory Deception: ESP, Psychics, Shirley MacLaine, Ghosts, UFOs . . . .* Buffalo: Prometheus Books.

Hansel, C. E. M. 1980. *ESP and Parapsychology—A Critical Re-Evaluation*. Buffalo: Prometheus Books.

Heftmann, Erica. 1982. *Dark Side of the Moonies*. Ringwood, Victoria, Australia: Penguin Books Australia.

Henderson, M. Allen. 1985. *Flim-Flam Man: How Con Games Work*. Boulder, CO: Paladin Press.

————. 1986. *Money for Nothing: Rip-Offs, Cons and Swindles*. Boulder, CO: Paladin Press.

Herbert, Victor, M.D., J.D. 1980. *Nutrition Cultism—Facts and Fictions*. Philadelphia: George F. Stickley Company.

Herbert, Victor ,M.D., J.D., and Stephen Barrett, M.D. 1981. *Vitamins & "Health" Foods: The Great American Hustle*. Philadelphia: George F. Stickley Company.

Hitler, Adolph. [1925] 1971. *Mein Kampf (My Battle)*. Boston: Houghton Mifflin Company.

Hoffer, Eric. 1951. *The True Believer*. New York: Harper & Row

Houdini, Harry. 1906. *The Right Way to Do Wrong: An Exposé*. Boston: Harry Houdini.

————. [1920] 1981. *Miracle Mongers And Their Methods*. Buffalo: Prometheus Books.

————. [1924] 1972. *Houdini: A Magician Among the Spirits*. New York: Arno Press.

Ireland, Laurie. [1938] 1963. *Lessons in Dishonesty*. Chicago: Magic, Inc.

James, H. K. 1914. *The Destruction of Mephisto's Greatest Web, Or, All Grafts Laid Bare*. Salt Lake City: The Raleigh Publishing Co.

Jarvis, William T. 1983. *Quackery and You*. Washington: Review and Herald Publishing Association.

Jerome, Lawrence E. 1977. *Astrology Disproved*. Buffalo: Prometheus Books.

Karrass, Chester L. 1974. *Give & Take: The Complete Guide to Negotiating Strategies and Tactics*. New York: Thomas Y. Crowell.

Keene, M. Lamar. 1976. *The Psychic Mafia*. New York: Dell Publishing Co., Inc.

Korem, Dan. 1988. *Powers: Testing the Psychic & Supernatural*. Downers Grove, IL: InterVarsity Press.

Kurtz, Paul, Editor. 1985. *A Skeptics Handbook of Parapsychology*. Buffalo: Prometheus Books.

Kusche, Lawrence David. 1975. *The Bermuda Triangle Mystery Solved*. New York: Warner Books.

Lampkin, Al. 1973. *Cheating at Cards*. Alhambra, CA: Alhambra Publishing Co.

Landers, Ann. 1978. *The Ann Landers Encyclopedia*. Garden City, NY: Doubleday & Company, Inc.

Lowell, James A. 1987. *Health Hoaxes and Hazards*. Tucson: Nutrition Information Center.

Lucas, Netley. 1927. *Ladies of the Underworld*. New York: J. H. Sears & Company, Inc.

MacDougall, Michael and J. C. Furnas. 1939. *Gamblers Don't Gamble*. New York: Garden City Publishing Co., Inc.

Mackay, Charles. [1841] 1980. *Extraordinary Popular Delusions and the Madness of Crowds*. New York: Harmony Books.

Marks, David and Richard Kammann. 1980. *The Psychology of the Psychic*. Buffalo: Prometheus Books.

Maurer, David W. 1974. *The American Confidence Man*. Springfield, IL: Charles C. Thomas.

Michelmore, Peter. 1989. "Beware the Health Hucksters."
Reader's Digest. January 1989. Pleasantville, NY: The
Reader's Digest Association, Inc.

National Association of Bunco Investigators. 1985. *National
Association of Bunco Investigators Handbook.* Baltimore:
National Association of Bunco Investigators.

Newman, Susan. 1985. *Never Say Yes to a Stranger.* New
York: The Putnam Publishing Group.

Nolen, William A., M.D. 1974. *Healing: A Doctor in Search of
a Miracle.* New York: Random House.

Nomi, Toshitaka and Alexander Besher. [1983] 1988. *You Are
Your Blood Type.* New York: Pocket Books.

Ortiz, Darwin. 1984. *Gambling Scams.* New York: Dodd,
Mead & Company.

Popper, Karl R. 1963. *Conjectures and Refutations: The
Growth of Scientific Knowledge.* New York: Harper & Row,
Publishers.

Proskauer, Julien J. 1932. *Spook Crooks!* New York: A. L. Burt
Company.

————. 1946. *The Dead Do Not Talk.* New York: Harper &
Brothers Publishers.

Rachleff, Owen S. 1971. *The Occult Conceit: A New Look at
Astrology, Witchcraft & Sorcery.* New York: Bell Publishing
Company.

Radner, Sidney H. 1957. *How to Spot Card Sharps and their
Methods.* New York: Key Publishing Company.

Randi, James. [1975] 1982. *The Truth About Uri Geller.*
Buffalo: Prometheus Books.

————. [1980] 1982. *Flim-Flam! Psychics, ESP, Unicorns
and other Delusions.* Buffalo: Prometheus Books.

————. 1987. *The Faith Healers.* Buffalo: Prometheus Books.

Reiser, Martin, Louise Ludwig, Susan Saxe, and Clare
Wagner. 1979. "An Evaluation of the Use of Psychics in the
Investigation of Major Crimes." *Journal of Police Science
and Administration.* March 1979. Gaithersburg, MD.:
International Association of Chiefs of Police, Inc.

Richardson, John A., M.D. & Patricia Griffin, R.N. 1977.
Laetrile Case Histories. New York: Bantam Books, Inc.

Ruthchild, Miriam. 1978. *Cashing in on the Psychic*. Pomeroy, OH: Lee Jacobs Productions.

Santoro, Victor. 1988. *Frauds, Rip-Offs and Con Games*. Port Townsend, Washington: Loompanics Unlimited.

Scarne, John. 1956. *The Amazing World of John Scarne*. New York: Crown Publisher, Inc.

————. 1966. *The Odds Against Me: An Autobiography*. New York: Simon and Schuster.

Schiff, Irwin and Howy Murzin. 1982. *How Anyone Can Stop Paying Income Taxes*. Hamden, CT: Freedom Books.

Scot, Reginald. [1584] 1972. *The Discoverie of Witchcraft*. New York: Dover Publications, Inc.

Select Committee on Aging, House of Representatives. 1984. *Quackery: A $10 Billion Scandal*. Washington: U. S. Government Printing Office.

Silva, José. 1977. *The Silva Mind Control Method*. New York: Pocket Books.

Smith, Lindsay E. & Bruce A. Walstad. 1989. *Sting Shift: The Street-Smart Cop's Handbook of Cons and Swindles*. Littleton, CO: Street-Smart Communications.

Sorrows, Gene. 1985. *All About Carnivals*. North Miami: American Federation of Police.

Steiner, Robert A. 1973. *Mommy and Daddy Have Separated: A Primer for Children*. El Cerrito, CA: Penseur Press.

————. 1986. "Exposing the Faith-Healers." *The Skeptical Inquirer*. Fall 1986. Buffalo: CSICOP.

Stowers, Carlton. 1982. *The Unsinkable Titanic Thompson*. Burnet, Texas: Eakin Press.

The Tribune. 1988. *The World Almanac and Book of Facts*. New York: Pharos Books.

U. S. Department of Health and Human Services, Public Health Service, Food and Drug Administration. 1980. *The Big Quack Attack: Medical Devices*. Washington: U. S. Department of Health and Human Services.

United States Postal Inspection Service. 1979. *Take a Bite Out of Crime*. Washington: U. S. Postal Inspection Service.

Valentine, Tom. 1973. *Psychic Surgery*. Chicago: Henry Regnery Company.

Van Buren, Abigail. 1988. "Dear Abby." June 6, 1988. San Francisco: *San Francisco Chronicle*.

Waite, Arthur Edward. 1971. *The Pictorial Key to the Tarot*. New York: Multimedia Publishing Corp.

Walsh, Audley V. *John Scarne Explains Why You Can't Win—A Treatise on Three Card Monte and Its Sucker Effects*. [Publication date and data were not in the book.]

Weldon, S. James. 1980. *Twenty Years a Fakir*. Las Vegas: GBC Press.

Wood, G. Congdon and Birdie M. Presley. 1980. "The Cruelest Killers: An Update." *The Health Robbers*. Philadelphia: George F. Stickley Company.

RESOURCES

Bay Area Skeptics, 4030 Moraga, San Francisco, CA 94122.

Better Business Bureau—Consult your local telephone directory for the office nearest you.

The Committee for the Scientific Investigation of Claims of the Paranormal (CSICOP), Box 229, Buffalo, NY 14215.

Consumer Fraud Division—Consult your local District Attorney's Office.

Federal Trade Commission, 6th Street and Pennsylvania Avenue, N.W., Washington, DC 20580.

The National Association of Bunco Investigators, Inc., 400 East Pratt Street, Suite 800, Baltimore, MD 21202.

The National Council Against Health Fraud, Inc., Box 1276, Loma Linda, CA 92354.

Public Library. The Public Library can be extremely helpful in researching almost anything. It is an underused resource of enormous potential.

United States Food and Drug Administration (FDA), Rockville, MD 20857.

United States Postal Inspection Service, Washington, DC 20260-2186, OR, consult your local U. S. Post Office.

Your first contact, when in doubt, when anything strikes you as suspicious, or just to be directed to the proper source of information or law enforcement—Contact your local Police Department. *Do not delay!*

ADDENDA

ABOUT THE AUTHOR

Bob is committed to exposing fraud and educating the public about con artists. He pursues this goal in a number of ways, but most of all through his skill as a performing magician, which he uses not only to entertain but to challenge irrational thinking.
Meredy Amyx (Amyx 1988, 8).

Bob Steiner is a CPA, professional magician, psychic and bunco investigator, and a quackbuster. He brings an interesting perspective to his investigations. He can duplicate or explain virtually all of the bunco and bunkum.

At universities and public demonstrations, he has convinced substantial portions of his audience that he has psychic powers. Later he tells them it was bunkum, and that it was all done by trickery. At medical conferences, he demonstrates the so-called psychic surgery, then explains its fraudulent nature. At law enforcement seminars, he distributes play money—Bunco Bucks™, then wins it back by cheating. The participants accept as a rule of the game that they will bet and try to win. That allows them to experience just a bit of how it feels to be taken by a con.

Bob's credentials include:

- National President 1988-1989, The Society of American Magicians
- Fellow of The Committee for the Scientific Investigation of Claims of the Paranormal (CSICOP)
- Member of The National Association of Bunco Investigators
- On the Board of Directors of the National Council Against Health Fraud
- Founder, Past Chair, and Advisor of Bay Area Skeptics

203

- Chair of the Occult Investigation Committee, The Society of American Magicians
- Member of The Academy of Magical Arts (Hollywood Magic Castle)
- Member of The Magic Circle
- Member of The International Brotherhood of Magicians
- Member of The Pacific Coast Association of Magicians
- Member of several other magic organizations.

REACTIONS TO STEINER'S PRESENTATIONS

In addition to being a lot of fun, your presentation demonstrated how surprisingly easy it is to fall for phony miracles that medical quacks use to sell their dangerous nonsense. The feedback we received was excellent; you were a hit.

Andrew Skolnick
Associate Science News Editor
American Medical Association

His being a skilled professional conjurer as well as an experienced public speaker and performer makes him extremely effective—in a way that almost no professor could be, especially in helping audiences separate genuine claims from charlatanry. For example, he actually demonstrates how easy it is for anyone to be fooled by doing just that. He fools everyone and entertains the audience in the process. In my Critical Judgment Seminar, he did a beautiful segment exposing many of the deceptions employed in organized and white collar crime.

Professor John W. Patterson
Iowa State University

I would like to extend our sincere appreciation for the outstanding presentation you made to our organization. Your knowledge and enthusiasm made for a truly substantial learning experience for all in attendance. Your presentation was not only very entertaining, but very informative as well.

Mary Ellen Bray
Peninsula Region
California Crime Prevention Officers Association

Your magical abilities to enthrall and involve an audience with feats that have value and purpose and relate to our profession was a theme-setting highlight; your psychic surgery demonstration caused gasps and created wonderment for even the most hard-boiled and pessimistic surgeons in the audience; and your third contribution—your warm and personable charm and enthusiasm—helped you to befriend and be befriended by dozens of participants, which made the purpose of your time with us all that much more valuable.

Brad Davis, Executive Director
The Multnomah County (OR) Medical Society

For information about presentations by Bob Steiner, please write to:

Bob Steiner
c/o Wide-Awake Books
Box 659
El Cerrito, CA 94530

Please send ____ copies of *DON'T GET TAKEN!*

____ copies @ $14.95 $_____

Postage and handling:
$2 for one copy; $4 for two or more copies   _____

California residents please add sales tax   _____

    Total $_____

Send check or money order to:

WIDE-AWAKE BOOKS
Box 659
El Cerrito, CA 94530

Name _____

Address _____

City_____ State____ Zip_____

For information about presentations by Bob Steiner, please write to:

Bob Steiner
c/o Wide-Awake Books
Box 659
El Cerrito, CA 94530

Please send ＿＿＿ copies of *DON'T GET TAKEN!*

＿＿＿ copies @ $14.95 $＿＿＿＿＿

Postage and handling:
$2 for one copy; $4 for two or more copies   ＿＿＿＿＿

California residents please add sales tax   ＿＿＿＿＿

   Total $＿＿＿＿＿

Send check or money order to:

WIDE-AWAKE BOOKS
Box 659
El Cerrito, CA 94530

Name ＿＿＿＿＿＿＿＿＿＿＿＿＿＿＿＿＿＿＿＿＿＿＿

Address ＿＿＿＿＿＿＿＿＿＿＿＿＿＿＿＿＿＿＿＿＿

City＿＿＿＿＿＿＿＿＿ State＿＿＿ Zip＿＿＿＿＿＿

For information about presentations by Bob Steiner, please write to:

Bob Steiner
c/o Wide-Awake Books
Box 659
El Cerrito, CA 94530

Please send _____ copies of *DON'T GET TAKEN!*

_____ copies @ $14.95 $_____

Postage and handling:
$2 for one copy; $4 for two or more copies   _____

California residents please add sales tax   _____

    Total $_____

Send check or money order to:

WIDE-AWAKE BOOKS
Box 659
El Cerrito, CA 94530

Name _____

Address _____

City_____ State_____ Zip_____

36